SOCIAL WORK ETHICS

SOCIAL WORK ETHICS

Charles S. Levy, D.S.W.
Wurzweiler School
of Social Work,
Yeshiva University

 **HUMAN SCIENCES PRESS**
72 Fifth Avenue   3 Henrietta Street
NEW YORK, NY 10011 ● LONDON, WC2E 8LU

To the memory of Dr. William A. Rosenthal,
late dean of the Wurzweiler School of Social Work,
Yeshiva University.

Copyright © 1976 by Human Sciences Press
72 Fifth Avenue, New York, New York 10011

Paperback Edition 1979

Printed in the United States of America
9 9876543

Library of Congress Cataloging in Publication Data

Levy, Charles
Handbook of Social Work Ethics

LC 75-11007
ISBN: 0-87705-493-2
ISBN: 0-87705-254-9

CONTENTS

PREFACE

A funny thing happened to me on the way to this book:
I rediscovered myself. I also changed.

Anyone who can say this when well into his middle
years must be grateful to many persons and many institutions. And I am. I will not be able to name all of them; nor
are they all still with us. Wherever they are, if I neglect to
name them they should share whatever credit is accorded
to me. But they are free of any blame for what I have done;
that is my own responsibility.

I must specify, within the brief space allotted me for
the purpose, a few of those persons and places that have
been important to this book and to me. The first of these
are the University of Toronto School of Social Work and
its former director, Dr. Charles E. Hendry. The school was
a gracious and undemanding setting in which to coddle my
curiosity and stimulate my inquisitiveness about the complex but intriguing arena of occupational ethics. The
school and the university asked nothing of me but to relax,
be present, and enjoy the pursuit of my inquiry—the choice
of which they left entirely to me. But they did afford me
exquisite resources and the great value that is associated
with refreshing encounters with interested and interesting
people. They also facilitated my endeavor.

Dr. Hendry knew long ago that a book like this must
be written, but neither his invitation on behalf of the Harry
Cassidy Memorial Research Fund nor his transactions and

contacts with me during the course of that most memorable year I spent at the University of Toronto carried any implication of an expected outcome. He was content to leave me to my own devices and in fact help me with them.

His successor, Dr. Albert Rose, continued to be interested and helpful, as were the entire faculty and staff of the School of Social Work, among whom I must mention Mrs. Florence Strakhovsky, research secretary of the Cassidy Fund.

Dr. Morton I. Teicher, former dean of the Wurzweiler School of Social Work, Yeshiva University, and now dean of the School of Social Work of the University of North Carolina, was also most encouraging and helpful. And Dr. Samuel Belkin, president of Yeshiva University, was an inspiration.

Colleagues at the Wurzweiler School of Social Work have been important to me, and frequent interaction with a number of them did much to help me crystallize many of the ideas in this book.

I do not see how the book could have been written, in the circumstances under which it has been written, without the skillful help of Mrs. Helen L. Nunes of the Wurzweiler School staff. Suffering through my atrocious handwriting, she promptly and diligently typed each section of the manuscript as I delivered it. This proved essential in sustaining the thread of my own interest (I still consider the processing of a manuscript a nuisance, although I relish the writing of works that interest me) and in sustaining what I hope will be perceived as the thread of the book's continuity.

I certainly owe my wife, Faye, a word of thanks, if not of apology, for I have constantly clogged our dining room table with books and notes and have obviously interfered with her life and opportunities. Although I can return the dining room table to her, I cannot recapture her lost time and opportunity. I hope at least that she enjoyed as much as I did my digressions from my task to discuss with her the thoughts that it evoked in me. My daughters, Barrie Pundyk and Helena Stern, as well as their husbands, Joseph and Stuart respectively, also gave me many opportunities to discuss my ideas with them and generated my interest in exploring those ideas further.

I am especially grateful to Mrs. Mary Gottesfeld, who presented to the publisher and to me the idea of writing this book, and to Norma Fox, editor-in-chief of Human Sciences Press, who nurtured it into being.

Before I end this acknowledgment, I must refer to my mother, Mollie Valenci Levy, and my late father, Hyman Levy, whose very victimization by unethical conduct—not simply thievery or other blatantly unethical acts but also sheer insensitivity, exploitation, and neglect—during some devastating years may have been the genesis of my interest in the subject of this book. Until I sat down to write the book, I do not believe I realized how pervasive and enduring a motif ethics has been in my life. In this respect, writing the book has represented a process of integration, so I cannot help but be grateful.

Finally, although it is not without embarrassment that I have borrowed so freely from my own published articles in a number of professional journals, it is really my way of saying "thank you" to these publications for they represented that essential "listening ear" which encouraged my quest for understanding and afforded an arena for sharing such understanding as I thought I had acquired. Without them, I doubt that this book could have happened.

Charles S. Levy
New York, 1975.

ACKNOWLEDGMENTS

Many sources were obviously tapped in the preparation of this book, for all of which I am profoundly indebted. I would like to express my particular thanks to *Social Work,* the Journal of the National Association of Social Workers, for permission to adapt "The Context of Social Work Ethics," Vol. 17, No. 2, (March, 1972), pp. 95–101; "The Ethics of Supervision," Vol. 18, No. 2, (March, 1973), pp. 14–21; and "On the Development of a Code of Ethics," Vol. 19, No. 2, (March, 1974), pp. 207–18; and for permission to paraphrase a portion of Seymour L. Halleck, "The Impact of Professional Dishonesty on Behavior of Disturbed Adolescents," Vol. 8, No. 2, (April, 1963), pp. 48–56.

I would also like to thank the *Journal of Jewish Communal Service* for permission to adapt "Labor-Management Relations in the Jewish Community Center," Vol. 41, No. 1, (Fall, 1964), pp. 114–123, and "The Relevance (or Irrelevance) of Consequences to Social Work Ethics," Vol. 51, No. 1, (Fall, 1974), pp. 73–81.

I would like to thank as well *Social Casework,* Journal of the Family Service Association of America, for permission to adapt "Values and Planned Change," Vol. 53, No. 8, (October, 1972), pp. 488–493; and *Social Service Review* for permission to adapt "Advocacy and the Injustice of Justice," Vol. 48, No. 1, (March, 1974), pp. 39–50.

My thanks also to *Psychotherapy: Theory, Research and*

Practice, for permission to quote from D. A. Begelman, "The Ethics of Behavioral Control and a New Mythology," Vol. 8, No. 2, (Summer, 1971), pp. 165–169; and to John Wiley and Sons, Inc., for permission to quote from John W. Thibaut and Harold H. Kelley, *Social Psychology of Groups* (1959).

Chapter 1

INTRODUCTION:
SOCIAL WORK ETHICS?

How can work that is "social" be anything but "ethical"? This question becomes especially compelling when one remembers that social workers have often been described as do-gooders. How can do-gooders be anything but ethical? More than almost any other human service occupation, social work seems to be implicitly ethical. The work that social workers do, the reasons they do it, and the way they do it are quite consistently unselfish (Cf. Addams, 1964). In fact, social workers have been characterized as "professional altruists" (Lubove, 1965). By definition, their work entails the well-being of others, individually and collectively. And unselfishness and altruism would certainly be included among the significant hallmarks of professional ethics. Therefore, why social work ethics?

One measure of ethical conduct in any occupation is the discrepancy between what its practitioner is supposed to do and what he actually does—assuming he has the competence to do it. The more these coincide, the more ethical the practice. The problem, however, is that what the social worker is supposed to do is not always evident and the measures of deviation are rarely precise. Far too many interests are affected, and far too many variables must be contended with. This is at once the reason why social work ethics is necessary and why it is so unwieldy. Many social workers do many things with many persons under numerous circumstances. Aside from the knowledge and skill required to do these things, guidelines are needed if they are to be done ethically, or at least if sufficient account is to be taken of the ethical issues they pose. Although all the interests affected by an ethical issue in a practice experience cannot invariably be reconciled, ethical practice requires that they be satisfactorily reckoned with, not so much in quest of what may be considered a successful outcome as in fulfillment of ethical responsibility. Competent practice is addressed to the efficient; ethical practice is addressed to the obligatory.

What social workers do is based on values—that is, on what social workers regard as preferably done. How it is done is also based on values—preferences concerning the ways of doing what is done (Levy, 1973e). To prefer a particular end and to prefer a way of attaining it is not the same as contending with what amounts to moral obligations when considering and acting on these preferences. Preferences—or values—have to be clear, however, if they are to serve as a reliable basis for action. Ethics, in effect, is values in operation.

In short, social work ethics needs some sorting out. That is the purpose of this book. To the extent that this purpose can be accomplished, it is not done at all prematurely. As a profession, social work has never been more complex, nor has it ever been in greater need of an explicit ethical formulation. The professional association of social workers does have a code of ethics (see "Profession of

Social Work"), but it is preambular in nature and does not reflect the complexity that generally characterizes ethical issues in professional practice.

One of the challenges in any attempt to explicate the considerations and strictures affecting ethical practice in social work is the vast range of activities included in the profession's scope. Social workers counsel individuals who suffer everything from income deficiencies or debilitating depressions to difficulties in their relationships with other persons or their families or problems of readjusting to community life after an appreciable regimen of institutional (medical, correctional, or psychiatric) living. Social workers "treat" families that are in conflict or in the process of adapting to the needs of one or another of their members. Social workers assist groups in attaining satisfaction, in enriching their personal growth, or in anticipating problems of social adjustment. By way of committees, organizations, and other media, social workers help communities and community groups to plan and allocate resources and to cope with social conditions and attempt to change them. Social workers administer social agencies and guide staff members and others through complex administrative processes. Social workers conduct research, and they teach in social work schools. There is little that social workers do not do, and they do what they do with all kinds of persons of all ages and descriptions and under all kinds of conditions. Sometimes they use different names and labels to describe what they do—social work, social casework, social group work, community social work, administration, counseling, psychotherapy; yet there is an occupational tie that binds them. There are also organizational ties which bind those who affiliate with professional associations identified with social work. Despite the range of their activities and the variations in emphases in the ways they are described and conceptualized, social workers share an occupational identity to a considerable extent and are guided by similar principles of practice. The objective of this effort is to find such a common denominator in ethical principles.

Another challenge in this effort is the wide range of backgrounds represented among persons who can be said to be practicing social work or who call themselves social workers. Licensing and certification in a number of jurisdictions notwithstanding, there are persons doing what can be called social work in some form who have less than a bachelor's degree—any bachelor's degree—or have a bachelor's degree in social work, a master's degree in social work of some kind, or a doctoral degree in social work, social welfare, or some other field.

Many social workers have undergone a program of education or training in which socialization into social work ideology figures as a prominent and explicit intention. Many have not. The prospect of a common foundation of ethical principles, however indefinitive, that is derived from or applicable to so disparate a group of practitioners with such a disparate array of job functions is apt to be limited. And yet the attempt must be made since the social work profession does exist, thousands of practitioners do identify themselves with it, and millions of persons are affected by it.[1]

What is required, especially in view of the diffusiveness of the social work profession and the diversity of its practitioners and their practices, is a systematic framework for the decisions that practitioners make when they encounter ethical issues in their practice. The nature of these issues will obviously have to be clarified, and some distinction will have to be made between them and other kinds of practice issues. All ethical issues require action choices of some kind. The social worker must decide what to do at certain

---

[1]The status of social work as a profession and the consequences of that status for social work ethics are discussed in Chapter 3.

junctures and under particular circumstances—whether to act, speak, be silent, or gesticulate, and so on—depending on whether he is addressing a client's or group's need or response, conforming to an agency's policy or function, trying to advance a professional objective, or whatever.

The essential difference between practice issues and ethical issues is that the latter arise, not so much from the need to get a particular job done as from concern about some risk to or right of the social worker's clientele or others that is incidental, but nevertheless critical, to the job being done. Such risks and rights, among other stakes associated with ethical issues, will also be considered. Perhaps it will suffice for the moment to say that a modicum of competence for social work practice of any kind must be assumed before ethical issues can be contended with. Without the basic ability to do the job that the social worker is engaged to do, the social worker can hardly exercise choice concerning the manner in which he will do it, whether to fulfill professional responsibility, or to avoid infringing on the rights of his clientele, or to effect some other moral consequence in the process.

This emphasis on the rights of the social worker's clientele may seem unduly ominous in view of the generally beneficent nature of social work and the general tendency of social workers to be honest and benevolent to a fault—certainly as compared with many other occupations. Instances of embezzlement and exploitation among social workers are relatively rare. It may also be true that their opportunities are also relatively rare; hence, aside from problems of inadequate reporting that afflict many spheres of modern life, the comparatively low incidence of hanky-panky among social workers. Perhaps. The likelihood is greater that because of its very nature as a profession suffused with social aspirations and one highly congruent with a social ethic, it attracts persons with an ethical bent.

An ethical bent does not automatically produce an ethical social worker, however: not because the social worker loses his ethical inclination (although that is not entirely inconceivable) but partially at least because the ethical issues that arise in social work practice are rarely if ever one-dimensional. In confrontations with ethical issues in their daily practice, social workers usually want to be ethical, but sometimes they do not know how, or they sometimes find themselves temperamentally or constitutionally unable to be.

Then, of course, in the spirit of benevolence with which social workers sometimes feel cloaked, they cannot at times conceive of themselves as being unethical—at times. A do-gooder (and this is not said invidiously, though the term is usually used disparagingly, for "doing good" is hardly reprehensible), a do-gooder who does "good" and knows it and often does so at some self-sacrifice is not given to suspecting his motives. He is in a position to know that he is not accruing inordinate rewards for his efforts, certainly not at the disproportionate expense of his clientele, and he can usually guess whether he is being helpful, especially if he knows what he is doing. If he is ever attentive to the needs of his clientele, he is not likely to err.

But that is the error! As Kant (1963) analagously cautioned: "The most ungodly of all passions is that of religious fervour, because it makes man think that under the cloak of piety he can do all manner of things [p. 147]." It is sometimes difficult for a social worker to question his actions when they are sincerely taken for the client's "own good."

Ethics transcends good work and good practice. And there may be more at stake than meets the social worker's naked eye—for the client (whether individual, group, agency, or community), for society, and for others, to any and all of whom the social worker may owe ethical homage. This too requires illumination.

It is not only the potentially harmful consequences of

unethical practice that make social work ethics especially significant. It is also the important work that social workers do and the great need that clienteles often have for them to do it that make social work ethics imperative.

Social workers can do work, and they have work to do that requires doing if the comfort and well-being of many persons, and perhaps of society, are to be carefully safe-guarded. The comfort and well-being of these persons, and perhaps of society, are often entrusted to social workers by means of licensing, certification, or other forms of sanction that permit social workers considerable freedom to prac-tice. In view of this, many persons and groups resort to these same social workers for help and further entrust their comfort and well-being to them. If the social workers fail or willfully neglect to provide the help that these persons seek and have been led to expect they can get from the social workers, they are not only depriving these persons of the help they need but preventing them from receiving it somewhere else. But these persons may need the help so badly that they may not even be in a position to judge whether they are being given short shrift. In fact, they may be in such dire straits that they become easy marks for, and quite helpless when confronted with social workers who have any inclination toward negligence, laziness, or sheer exploitation for the sake of their own personal gain, gratifi-cation, or self-aggrandizement.

The social workers may be perfectly capable of doing what they are supposed to do and what their clienteles require. Whether they do it or not, in what manner, and at what penalty to their clienteles and others—these are ethi-cal issues, and ethical issues are what this book is primarily about.

Chapter 2

SOCIAL WORK ETHICS AS PROFESSIONAL ETHICS

The purpose of this chapter is not to certify social work's status as a profession. Consideration will have to be given later to those attributes that social work does share with other occupations more confidently classified as professions, but it will be done primarily to examine the bearing these attributes have on social work ethics.[1]

This statement is made in the spirit that evidently guided Carr-Saunders and Wilson (1964), whose report on their investigation of professions remains a classic in the literature on the subject:

> It is no part of our purpose to attempt to draw a line between professions and other vocations; we are not concerned to say what vocations are professions and what are not. We are therefore absolved from the necessity of examining all those vocations which claim professional rank in order that we

[1]As recently as 1972, social work was classified as a "semi-profession" (Toren, 1972).

may decide upon their true position. Indeed, the drawing of a boundary line would be an arbitrary procedure, and we shall not offer, either now or later, a definition of professionalism. Nevertheless when we have completed our survey, it will emerge that the typical profession exhibits a complex of characteristics, and that other vocations approach the condition more or less closely, owing to the possession of some of their characteristics fully or partially developed [pp. 3–4].

The primary concerns here are the extent to which standards of conduct, attributable to professions—and particularly human service professions—are applicable to social work and the distinctiveness of these standards of conduct compared with standards of conduct expected of persons in everyday life.[2] Specifically, what is of interest here is how and why social work ethics differs from ethics in general. An understanding of professional ethics is essential for the illumination of these questions, despite the tentativeness of the judgment sometimes expressed about the professional status of social work. Therefore, some discussion is necessary about the characteristics of social work that coincide with those of more fully accredited human service professions and lay the foundation for the discussion of social work ethics.

This foundation begins with the social work service situation. The social work service situation connects social worker and client—any kind of client, whether individual, group, community, or institution. The client needs, resorts to, or commissions a service that the social worker is ad-

[2]By human service professions is meant those occupations whose professional status is generally acknowledged and usually legally endorsed and which provide services of various kinds directly to persons, families, groups, committees, organizations, and institutions, usually on a face-to-face basis. These professions include medicine, psychiatry, psychology, law, nursing, teaching, the ministry, and other occupations for the practice of which societal sanction, learned competence, and a consumer stake of some consequence are assumed.

judged on some ground to be both qualified and accredited to render.[3] This service encompasses all that social worker and client do in relation to that service and includes not only the face-to-face encounters between them but all other acts and statements that pertain to or affect that service.

For the social worker, the social work service situation represents both a responsibility and an opportunity to provide the service his client seeks and makes possible. Therefore, presented here is what Pepper (1960) has described as

> a problematic situation [that], when carefully analyzed, furnishes its own criterion for the solution of the problem contained in it. . . . The ethical criterion for the rightness or wrongness of the act is the reality of the situation, its actual structure [pp. 139, 140].

The connection between social worker and client is initiated in a variety of ways. How it is initiated is itself a measure of the social worker's ethical responsibility. The elite board that engages the social worker to implement its deliberately chosen policies and programs is not as vulnerable to exploitation or abuse as is the client in crisis who desperately seeks the social worker's help, and the board is certainly not as hemmed in as is the client who is a client, not because he needs or wants to be, but because a court or a welfare department requires him to be: for example, the probationer, parolee, and applicant for public assistance, whose freedom or income is conditional on their subjection to social work service. All, however, rely on the social worker's good offices to advance their social work-related purposes and to avoid hampering them in attaining their ends.

When a client assigns the social worker a task, or when the social worker is assigned a task in his behalf—whether

[3]Some of this discussion is adapted from Levy (1972a).

payment is made by the client on terms he agrees to or by some private or governmental third party—the client invests himself in the social worker because of his expressed or assumed need and divests himself of other available alternatives.

When time or opportunity is of the essence in relation to the client's need (as it is apt to be in a crisis), a social worker's failure to apply himself to the client's need may mean the neglect of it or the deprivation of the client's access to whatever the need depends on.

The nature and the components of the social work service situation underscore what Max Weber (1946) described as the "ethics of responsibility," which demands accountability for the foreseeable results of the social worker's actions. The social worker obviously has some responsibility to provide for what he foresees as inherent in or a possible consequence of the social work service situation.

Whether or not social work is regarded as a fully developed profession, the social work service situation establishes the major ethical premise that when a client comes to the social worker for service for which the social worker himself or his employing agency, school of social work, or society itself, through a specific system of formal (i.e., legal) or informal sanctions, certifies his competence, the social worker is duty bound—that is, it is his ethical responsibility—to provide that service to the full measure of his expected competence. The social worker who is permitted and is perhaps certified or licensed by society—through legal certification or licensing, for example—to practice social work has the ethical responsibility to be competent as well as to perform competently because his clientele has been led to expect this of him. This expectation amounts to a first ethical principle because it leads to the social work service situation and the exposure to which the social worker's clientele is subjected as a result.

Social work ethics, however, should not be confused

with social work competence or the effectiveness of its application. As Begelman (1971) pointed out:

> There is no necessary relationship between ethics and effec-
> tiveness in any treatment procedure. Effectiveness cannot be
> the sole criterion of whether the procedure is ethical. Nei-
> ther do I believe that unethical procedures must inevitably
> be ineffective in alleviating behavioral problems [p. 165].

An ethical procedure is not necessarily effective. To the
contrary, this may be the very nature of a social worker's
conflict in coping with a service situation. His practice wisdom may inform him of a step calculated to be helpful to
his client, and yet he may, on ethical grounds, refrain from
taking it. He may, for example, "know," on the basis of
diagnostic sophistication and relevant experience, that his
client's marriage is destined to be destructive to him but
avoid intruding on the client's responsibility to make his
own choice and on his right to err. The first would be a
practice judgment; the latter, an ethical one. The first is
based on knowledge; the latter, on values. The client's
choice might well lead to an intensification of the very
problems that have directed him to the social worker. But
if the social worker values the client's option, he settles for
an ethical choice that proves to be an impractical one: i.e.,
an "ineffective" one from the vantage point of social work
practice. The choice amounts to unused competence in the
interest of applied ethics. The social worker's practice proficiency will be further constrained if, in addition, he believes it is incumbent on him—as a pious person if not as
a social worker—to preserve the family as a social or religious institution.

On the other hand, ethics can hardly be said to be
"secondary to technical proficiency," as Alfred Kadushin
(1959; p. 76) once put it. Ethics is a concurrent, not a
secondary consideration in social work practice. It is an-

other consideration, guided by other criteria and principles.

What is ethical is that which ought to be done, though it is not better done. And professional ethics signifies that which ought to be done in an occupational capacity because of the responsibility assumed to be carried by virtue of occupational capacity.

The characteristics of social work that have been emphasized and are related to the social work service situation and social work responsibility are similar in nature and consequence to those of the acknowledged human service professions. They identify the premises on which social work ethics can be built. For social work, as for the human service professions in general,

> the ethically "better" is equivalent to that which we "ought to do". . . . Since the failure to act in one manner is commonly set out against the choice of an alternative action, we are in a secondary way led to speak of that which we "ought to do," in distinction from that which we "ought not." In strictness . . . we are not under obligation to do a thing because it is better. . . . It is ethically better because we ought to do it [Rogers, 1922, p. 85].

What ought to be done by the social worker in a social work service situation is a function of his practice responsibility as a social worker. In this sense social work ethics is a special case of professional ethics, which is generally a function of practice responsibility. Professional ethics must be distinguished, however, from general ethics and other value-derived concepts that affect and guide human conduct, and serve as a basis for evaluating it.

What is expected of the social worker (and this applies to practitioners of all human service professions) is not expected of the man in the street. The expectations of both may of course coincide, but only because what is expected of the social worker may in some particulars also be expected of others. That is but happenstance, however, for what is expected of the social worker, beyond occupational competence, is expected because he is a social worker and he does social work. What is expected of others is what is expected of human beings in general because they are human beings. Thus, what is expected of human beings in general is also expected of social workers, for they too are human beings. But what is expected of social workers is not expected of human beings in general because not all human beings are social workers. It is true, however, that much that is expected of social workers is expected of human service practitioners in general, and much that is expected of human service practitioners in general is expected of social workers in particular. But the reason for this is that they have similar responsibilities to others.

What distinguishes professional ethics, as applied to human service practitioners in general and to social workers in particular, is the fact that it is not intended to describe personal qualities, whether in their own right or as stimuli to ethical conduct. This distinction was evidently Aristotle's intention in his discussion of "virtues" in "Nichomachean Ethics." He does assert that "to virtue belongs virtuous activity [p. 320], but in doing so he separates the quality of the person from the behavior it compels in him. He emphasizes this in fact by insisting that "intellectual virtue in the main owes both its birth and its growth to teaching . . . while moral virtue comes about as a result of habit [p. 331]," a word he associates etymologically with the Greek word for ethics. In short, these are personal qualities that are valued, whatever their possessors do with them, but there are acts that are valued which may or may not be outcomes or consequences of those qualities. These acts can be described as morals that, although not entirely consistent with past usage, are distinguishable from ethics: ethics in general, that is.

The concept ethics is limited here to conduct arising from specific interpersonal relationships: relationships between individuals and other persons, groups, and institutions or relationships among persons, groups, and institutions. Morals, on the other hand, describe acts that are valued in themselves or judged on their own merits without regard to obligations to others. They may correspond to norms of particular groups, communities, or societies, and deviations may be appraised and punished accordingly; but though they may affect others, their appraisal is not based on obligations to others attributed to perpetrators. Ethics and ethical responsibility do derive from such obligations. A deviation that may also be subject to sanctions represents a failure to fulfill such obligations.

The reason for stressing these distinctions is that they provide the key to the formulation of principles of professional ethics and the basis for discriminating judgments with regard to acts or omissions, either in or outside of one's occupational capacity. They can help as well to discourage moralistic judgments, which may serve perhaps in appraising the conduct of persons in general, when what is called for is objective evaluation of practitioners on the basis of clear and specifiable criteria of ethical judgment.

Clarification of the concept of ethics would help to clarify the concept of professional ethics since the latter is essentially a special case of the former. Melden (1959), in differentiating "obligatory" actions and "obligation-meeting" actions, identifies the first as arising from the "rights" of others [p. 51]. The determination of whether an action is "right," he explains, is conditioned "by the complex network of rights and obligations of the persons concerned and affected [p. 68]." He goes on to explore interpersonal relationships that illustrate such networks of mutual rights and obligations.

These relationships identify the variety of social and moral roles the participants play in the total community and in relation to one another and specify the diversity of their rights, privileges, and obligations in relation to those roles. Some of these rights, privileges, and obligations are "freely assumed and freely relinquished [p. 69]," but only when the relationship between participants can be altered at the will of one or another of them. But some relations are not so alterable at will. A husband or a parent, for example, is charged with roles (and hence the rights and obligations associated with them) that are

> not so freely relinquished, if at all, . . . [and thus] circum-scribe the area of legitimate choice. . . . The task of moral understanding in such cases is that of understanding the character of the action performed by viewing it in the context of the relevant rights and obligations of all of the parties concerned [Melden, 1959, pp. 69, 71].

Feinberg's (1961) threefold classification of duties and obligations includes a category that applies to Melden's description but states it in a form which is particularly germane to this discussion and broadens it as well. He refers to "the assigned tasks which 'attach' to stations, offices, jobs, and roles, which for some reason seem better named by the word 'duty' than by the word 'obligation' [p. 277]." He distinguishes this category from that of "duties of obedience," which "are actions required by laws and by authoritative command," and that of voluntary obligations, which are "actions to which we commit ourselves by making promises, borrowing money, making appointments, and so on [p. 277]." These classes of duties and obligations do not inhere in existing roles. The category of duties and obligations associated with stations and the like, on the other hand, is a function of specific roles. It augments the discussion of Melden's conception by including, along with roles imputed to participants in standing personal relationships, roles associated with vocational and occupational relationships.

Duties of obedience and voluntarily assumed commitment are also ethical in nature, but ethical responsibility is bounded by law or authoritative command in one case and by the specifically assumed commitment in the other. Duties associated with personal or occupational relationships, on the other hand, are inclusive constellations of obligation because they attach to the relationship and are defined by it. They are open-ended to the extent that the relationship itself makes possible. The ethical responsibility of participants is generated by that relationship. Whatever happens and whatever can happen in that relationship is what shapes the ethical responsibility of the participants.

Whatever its origins or impetus, ethics deals with standards or expectations of behavior and action (or inaction) in relation to others and arises out of some definition of individual or collective responsibility to others or for others. This responsibility is based on the nature of this relationship to others, whether personal, familial, social, or occupational (Levy, 1973a, p. 99).

The "rules" that govern the conduct (which is to say, the ethics) of human beings in their relationship to others are, as Durkheim (1958) saw it, of "two kinds":

> The first apply to all men alike. . . . These rules . . . are again divided into two groups: those concerning the relation of each one of us to his own self [compare discussion of virtues and morals above] . . . and those concerning the relations we maintain with other people . . . The obligations laid upon us by both the one and the other arise solely from our intrinsic human nature or from the intrinsic human nature of those with whom we find ourselves in relation. . . . But there are rules of one kind where the diversity is far more marked; they are those which taken together constitute professional ethics [pp. 3–4].

In the course of his quite remarkable (considering its dates: 1890–1900) analysis of the state of and need for professional ethics, Durkheim went on to observe: "A system of ethics . . . is not to be improvised. It is the task of the very group to which they are to apply [p. 13]."

Presumably, the task of systematizing the substance and operation of social work ethics is primarily that of social workers themselves. Certainly social workers are in a strategic position to appreciate the kinds of responsibilities they carry and the kinds of ethical issues these responsibilities engender. A great deal more must be known, considered, and done, however, before a full "system of ethics" can be developed and set into motion.

Chapter 3

WHAT ABOUT PROFESSIONALS MAKES PROFESSIONAL ETHICS SO NECESSARY?

For the intents and purposes of social work ethics, social work is a profession. Oh, it may not conform to every jot and tittle of the sociologists' paradigms, which presume to classify professions and distinguish them from semi-professions and nonprofessions; but in the ways that count for social work ethics, social work is a profession.

Anyone can arbitrarily set down any criteria he chooses to pass judgment on the professional status of any occupation, and there are such criteria. These criteria have been used to intimidate occupations, approve them, sanction them, and judge them. Such criteria have been used to set occupations hustling to satisfy them in quest of professional status.[1] But as far as social work ethics is concerned,

[1]It was evidently in response to this occupational inclination that Wilensky (1964) waggishly titled an article on the process of professionalization, "The Professionalization of Everyone?" "Many occupations," he observed, "engage in heroic struggles for professional identification; few make the grade [p. 137]."

these criteria are not particularly revealing or useful. For such a purpose, descriptive analyses of the characteristics of existing professions or near-professions are more useful than are projections of ideal-types as a kind of yardstick against which to rate occupations. Some devastating verses by e.e. cummings suggest a way of putting such paradigms in their place and permit a thoughtful consideration of the specific characteristics that describe social work as well as human service professions in general, including those that have passed muster in the critical eyes of sociologists:

> while you and i have lips and voices which
>   are for kissing and to sing with
> who cares if some oneeyed son of a bitch
>   invents an instrument to measure Spring with?
>   (voices to voices, lip to lip)

This is not to denigrate sociologists and paradigms. They do have their utility, but they do have to be put into perspective. The criteria that have been employed to classify occupations as professions have tended to rate them more in terms of their relationship to society and other occupations than in their relationship to those they serve, although the criteria of professional status do have implications for the clienteles of occupations so classified. The difficulty has been that occupational groups—social workers among them—have been so intent on attaining professional status for reasons of their own that they have sometimes neglected the reasons that affect their clienteles. And the criteria that have been emphasized have induced them to do it. As Hughes (1958) put it: "the concept 'profession' in our society is not so much a descriptive term as one of value and prestige" and "a symbol for a desired conception of one's work and, hence, of one's self [p. 44]."

It is as a descriptive term that the concept has relevance to social work and social work ethics. However, it is as a term connoting prestige and personal status that the concept has had a persevering influence on social workers for well over half a century. The concern of many social workers about their status has done much to prevent them from exploring the consequences of their professional status for their clienteles. Professional status does accord to occupations many privileges, which no doubt explains some of the zeal among practitioners to attain it. But especially important is the effect that such status has on those the practitioners serve, and this effect has sometimes been overlooked.

The agent provocateur who led social workers down the primrose path was Abraham Flexner. He proposed, in 1915, "certain objective standards" that might be employed as criteria of a profession. However, he was not content to let the matter rest there; he went on to make an immediate application of the criteria to social work and to conclude that "social work . . . appears not so much a definite field as an aspect of work in many fields [p. 585]." He considered social work too "vast" to make "delineation" possible, and delimitation or specialization of competence were, for him, prerequisites of professional status. "Would it not be at least suggestive therefore," he said, "to view social work as in touch with many professions rather than as a profession in and by itself [p. 586]?" Social workers as a group have not had a restful moment since. Much of what they did as an organized group between the 1920s and 1950s was calculated more to satisfy Flexner's criteria than to achieve substantive growth as a helpful occupation.

The irony in all this is that Flexner's criteria, like the criteria proposed by others since, relate more to where practitioners stand in society's hierarchies than to where their clienteles stand in relation to practitioners. To be a profession, Flexner insisted, (1) the activities of the occupation must be essentially intellectual in character—that is, "a free, resourceful, and unhampered intelligence" must be applied to problems, (2) the occupation must have a "learned character," dependent on a steady stream of ideas that keeps it from degenerating into mere routine and losing its intellectual and responsible character, (3) the occupation must be practical, not academic and theoretical, and its activities must be definite in purpose, (4) its principles, skills, and techniques must be capable of being communicated "through an orderly and highly specialized educational discipline," (5) its activities must "completely engage their votaries," and (6) organized groups of its members "are, under democratic conditions, apt to be more responsible to public interest than are unorganized or isolated individuals" (pp. 576–590).

Flexner did emphasize that under the pressure of public opinion, "professional groups have more and more tended to view themselves as organs contrived for the achievement of social ends rather than as bodies formed to stand together for the assertion of rights or the protection of interests and principles [p. 581]," but the fact remains that in fulfilling this criterion of professional status—that is, in organizing themselves into occupational groups—professions have indeed insured their own protection and even a monopoly in their practice.[2]

> Every profession strives to persuade the community to sanction its authority within certain spheres by conferring upon the profession a series of powers and privileges. . . . The powers and privileges . . . constitute a monopoly granted by the community to the professional group [Greenwood, 1957, p. 48–49].

From the community's point of view, professional status spells responsibility to others. From the practi-

[2]Wilensky (1964, pp. 144–145), whose analysis of professionalization coincides closely with Flexner's criteria, includes as phases in the process of professionalization the organization of local and national professional associations.

tioner's point of view, it spells privileges and protection as well as prestige. Benoit-Smullyan (1944) has provided a plausible explanation for the appeal of professional status to practitioners and the prestige it represents to them. The person of high prestige, he suggests (and there is little question that professional status accords a measure of prestige, more in some occupations than in others) is an object of admiration, an object of diffidence, an object of imitation, a source of suggestion, and a center of attraction. He goes on to caution that these attractions may not even be based on objective characteristics or personal achievements. In short, as applied to professions, prestige and its consequences are functions of professional status rather than qualities demonstrated by individual practitioners. Whatever its legislated professional status, social work—because of what it is and what it does as well as the circumstances under which it does what it does—incurs a degree of prestige and the responses of its clientele that prestige makes possible.

This striving to raise their prestige and its resultant rewards, which social workers like other practitioners have shown, is not without its dangers, among them "that the interests of the recipients [of service] can easily become subverted to serve the interests of the dispensers [Rein, 1964, p. 5]." And a former president of the National Association of Social Workers could not help but ask in a related context: "Are we truly interested in improved public service or are we looking forward to basking in the sun of respectability [Reichert, 1965, p. 140]?"

Professional status is a basis for the acquisition of respectability, but what it should connote first and foremost is the protection of clienteles. This protective base is needed by the social worker's clientele as much as by the clienteles of all the fully accredited human service professions because of the characteristics that social work shares with them.

Professional status is often a prerequisite for the privilege (or right) to engage in acts of service, and evidence of competence is a prerequisite for the status. Not infrequently, however, the competence and integrity essential to the service are assumed in the status and even in the position to render the service. A social worker doing social work—especially in an institutional setting, which is where most social workers do their social work—is usually assumed to have the necessary competence and integrity and often a great deal more besides. If there is insufficient basis for the assumption, the client has little choice but to resort to hope, unless he is free and un-needy enough to escape.

The operative features of social work, whether or not judicial, statutory, or sociological notice is taken of its professional status, are what ultimately counts in the definition of the social worker's ethical responsibility. The law, particularly case law, has made this especially evident. Usually deriving conclusions about professional status from facts and searching out the empirical foundations of behavioral expectations, legal decisions have emphasized the circumstantial premises for defining ethical responsibility. Even when these decisions discuss occupations other than social work, their facts often describe social work as well, and to that extent their conclusions about ethical responsibility also apply to social work. The law has made clear that it is not what practitioners have been called, or what they have been franchised to do, or the steps they have taken to acquire status or control but what they actually do in their occupational capacity which determines their obligations to their clientele. And what the cases describe other practitioners as doing that leads to judgments about ethical responsibility fits social workers in the most critical and decisive of connections. Fundamental in most cases is the principle that the limits on occupations as well as their license are not designed to protect the occupations but their clienteles (*People* v. *Alfani*, p. 673).

Although the case of *Meunier* v. *Bernich et al.* was concerned with the practice of law, it would take but minimal paraphrasing to apply it to social work as it is usually practiced and to reflect its implications for social work ethics:

> Clients need the services of the lawyer, not always for the purpose of litigation but for advice and counsel. Before the attorney gives his opinion, he examines the jurisprudence and advises the client to the best of his ability as to the question presented. . . . In most instances, the client, relying upon the lawyer's skill and training in the science of his profession, adopts the attorney's opinion as the final word respecting the client's right or liability. . . . Hence, for these reasons, aside from many others, the public is vitally interested in having only men of talent, ability and learning to serve it in legal matters [p. 572].

If anything, the process through which the social worker offers advice and counsel is far more complex than that which affects the lawyer and his client and makes all the more compelling the safeguards needed by the social worker's client, although the client's stake in both service situations is not always comparable. The ethical implications in both situations are, however. As the court admonished in *Baker* v. *Humphrey,* law, like medicine (and, one may add, like social work)

> may be potent for evil as well as good. Hence the importance of keeping it on the high plane it ought to occupy. Its character depends upon the conduct of its [practitioners]. . . . Their fidelity is guaranteed by the highest considerations of honor and good faith. . . . The slightest divergence from rectitude involves the breach of all these obligations. None are more honored or more deserving than those of the brotherhood who, uniting ability with integrity, prove faithful to their trusts and worthy of the confidence reposed in them [p. 502].

To social work, as to professions such as law and medicine, the "spirit of public service" is crucial (Pound, 1953, pp. 4–10). Gaining a livelihood, the main if not the only purpose of most callings, is incidental to it. Money-making does not represent a primary motivation for the practitioner. If "organization" and the pursuit of a learned art are to be regarded as being as essential for social work as they are for professions generally, it was Pound's view that they should be so regarded only to secure and maintain the spirit of public service. In other words, these attributes, like other attributes, are not functionally autonomous but rather are directly connected to the service mission of these occupations. And it is the service mission and the context of its implementation that prescribe their ethics.

Barber's (1963) enumeration of the essential attributes of professions, in terms of which professional behavior (including that of social workers in view of the descriptive and hence ethics-relevant connotations of the term) can be defined, becomes pertinent in this context. These attributes are a high degree of generalized and systematic knowledge, primary orientation to the community's interest rather than to individual self-interest, a high degree of behavioral self-control, and a system of rewards which is primarily a set of symbols of work achievement that are thus ends in themselves rather than means to some end of individual self-interest [p. 672]. The practitioner's interests in fact tend to depend on his serving the interests of his clients. His service to his clients "is presumed to depend on their need and not on their ability to pay" (Blau & Scott, p. 50).

The characteristics of professions that have been identified in law and literature, which seem to describe social work and point to obligations owed to social work clients and others affected by the social worker's practice, can be paraphrased as follows:

1. Social work is a calling or a vocation that requires special knowledge—knowledge that is relevant to the need for help, the kinds of help available, how people behave when seeking it, why they behave that way, and so forth.

2. Social work is an occupation that requires specific skills in helping people, in relating to them while doing so and in order to do so, and so on.

3. Social work involves special mental and other attainments or special discipline, such as the capacity to communicate orally and in writing, use oneself with the intention to render service, and the like.

4. Intellectual and practical education and training are available in graduate schools or university departments to prepare persons for the practice of social work.

5. The work that social workers do is practical work that incorporates and reflects knowledge and art and is applied to the affairs and needs of others by advising, guiding, and otherwise serving their interests or their welfare.

6. The skill that social workers employ is based on knowledge and principles rather than on techniques and rules of thumb applied on an ad hoc basis.

7. Social work is an intellectual rather than a manual art concerned with the production or sale of commodities.

8. Social work involves the application of special knowledge on behalf of others, and this knowledge is weighed in relation to each person to whom it is to be applied, as distinguished from pursuing it for one's own purposes.

9. Social workers are motivated by the goal of service rather than "money-getting" or profit-making, although they are compensated for the time and talent they employ in the service of others.

The needs of persons to which social workers address their efforts are characteristically needs that those persons cannot satisfy by themselves (O. Hall, 1961). This too is a feature that social work shares with professions. It effects the kind of hold on the social worker's clientele that makes a carefully calculated system of social work ethics indispensable if social work clienteles are not to be victimized by their needs or subjected to hazards associated with their quest for help with them.

The status of social workers in comparison with their clienteles, therefore, is very much a great unequalizer.[3] The social worker is, or is perceived by most clients to be in an advantageous position over them.

The relationship between the social worker and his clientele—individuals, groups, families, committees, organizations, and so on—is fairly consistently asymmetrical. The two not only behave differently, they are expected to act differently (Haley, 1963, p. 11). The social worker at least retains more jurisdiction over his autonomy than his clientele does over its own (Levy, 1973d). The more clients need the social worker's service, the less autonomous they are apt to feel and the less autonomously they are bound to act, unless the social worker compensates for this inclination. This becomes, then, a function of ethics for it affects less what the social worker does (as a matter of competence, for example) than how he does it. The preservation of the client's autonomy may be effected at the ex-

---

[3]This is obviously not a universal and standardized effect since some clienteles are in a more advantageous position than others. Still, the only difference is that of degree, so long as the clientele needs something and the social worker has it to give. On the other hand, the vast bulk of clients awaits the pleasure of the social worker, particularly, for example, welfare recipients and persons or families that are in crisis because of some personal or communal disaster or catastrophe. For them, the concept of status is not inconsequential. Benoit-Smullyan (1944) defined this concept as "relative position within a hierarchy," by which is meant "a number of individuals ordered on an inferiority-superiority scale with respect to the comparative degree to which they possess or embody some socially approved or generally desired attribute or characteristic [p. 151]."

pense of the solution to his problem or the satisfaction of his need. In this case, the social worker may be more responsive to his ethical responsibility than to his practice responsibility.

In these instances, the client may not be in a position to judge the validity of the social worker's action choice. Social work, no less than human service professions in general, is a specialized or "esoteric" service (Hughes, 1958, pp. 140–141). The client can only believe that the social worker "knows better," nor is he always capable of knowing whether the social worker's action is a response to his practice responsibility or his ethical responsibility. The former might well be more serviceable in relation to the client's need, but the latter might be more responsive to the social worker's moral obligations to the client.

The presumption of greater knowledge on the part of the social worker as compared with clients—another characteristic that is attributed to professions—is also antithetical to the clients' exercise of autonomy, even when availed of the opportunity to do so, and this too requires compensation through the implementation of ethical responsibility. Clients tend, in the face of the social worker's relative authority, to lose their capacity for autonomy as they incur the reluctance to exercise it. They tend to become dependent on that authority, and dependence is the enemy of autonomy (Emerson, 1962; Levy, 1963b).

Aside from the substantive advantage of the social worker's knowledge, which may humble clients, the assumption of the social worker's greater knowledge becomes a basis for demanding or inducing the kind of reliance that militates against the assertion of autonomy on the clients' part. What the social worker—like practitioners of human service professions in general—jeopardizes with his practice, competent though it may be, he must safeguard with his ethics.

The fact that social work is sanctioned by the community—another quality it shares with professions—is a basis for the trust of its clienteles. Implicit in this sanction is the "technical competence and moral integrity [Parsons, 1954, p. 155]" that frees clients to repose complete trust and confidence in the social worker. As Hughes (1958, pp. 141–142) has emphasized, a licensing system, for example, "adds the support of the state" to other means through which the profession can exercise control over clients and through which competence becomes "an attribute of the profession as a whole, rather than of individuals as such." This kind of sanction generates the "fiction that all licensed professionals are competent and ethical until found otherwise by their peers." Social work is sanctioned in this manner whether formally by license or otherwise, and is certainly accepted as a bona fide service occupation in the community at large, whether in a jurisdiction that licenses it or not.

To clients, community sanction means that social workers have been prescreened in terms of their integrity, ethics, and competence; thus it becomes unnecessary for clients to exercise their own judgment and restraint. When the social worker works in and for an agency, this inclination on the part of clients is reinforced because the situation implies not only community sanction but also agency sanction, which amounts to a second screening on the one hand and additional recourse on the other. Clients rely on the agency to choose its personnel carefully and underwrite or assume responsibility for the actions of its personnel.

Clients have little reason, in the absence of incontrovertible evidence to the contrary, to see things differently than social workers themselves have seen them. For example, a report by the National Association of Social Workers, "Utilization of Personnel in Social Work," points out that

one of the greatest strengths of social work today is the combination of inner and outer controls of worker behavior.

> Definition of agency function, policies and procedures guard against conscious or unconscious abuse of power and authority that may occur even in the most professionalized.

If social workers are so confident, why should clients be less so?

The accreditation of social workers having been effected as it has by the requirement and availability of professional education, training, and supervision—a further attribute of professions—clients are freer to rely on the social worker without fear of losing their own integrity.[4] The more they know about the objectives of the socialization process for social workers, the more cause they have for such reliance since the client and his options are highly valued in social work ideology. Clients can be confident that the social worker has been exposed to a regimen and is subject to authority that constrains him.

In effect the very nature of social work as an occupation dictates the need for a system of ethics specifically tailored for it. The details of the system stem from the relationship between social worker and clientele and perhaps others and the responses of each to the other in the course of giving and taking help. Social work's status in the community structures the framework for social work ethics. The social work service situation structures its operation. And it is to the social work service situation that we give our attention next.

[4]In his review of characteristics that make a community of a profession, Goode (1957) includes the following: "Though [a professional community] . . . does not produce the next generation biologically, it does so socially through its control over the selection of professional trainees, and through its training processes it sends these recruits through an adult socialization process [p. 194]," which of course includes the incorporation of the values shared by the profession. This applies in practice to social work.

Chapter 4

THE CONTEXT OF SOCIAL WORK
ETHICS

The most compellingly practical basis for defining the social worker's ethical responsibility toward his clients is the real-life situation in and through which he relates to them.[1] This does not mean, however, that more abstract or universal premises for defining ethical responsibility are not readily available. Codes of ethics frequently contain principles of professional conduct that are derived from broader systems of values and ethics, including philosophy and religion. The Code of Ethics of the National Association of Social Workers certainly contains such referents. Nevertheless, the service situation does provide the context for formulating principles of professional ethics that are specifically applicable to social work practice. The basis for defining the social worker's ethical responsibility and formulating guides for his ethical conduct may be obtained by focusing on the client and the experiences and responses

[1]This chapter is adapted from Levy, 1972a.

that are generated when he resorts to the social worker for help or service. It is not good conduct in universal terms that makes for ethical conduct in social work practice; it is behavior that is consonant with the requisites of the social work service situation.

To understand the nature of ethical responsibility and to identify guides to ethical conduct, the social work service situation must be scrutinized, especially to ascertain the obligations it implies for the social worker. The objective would be to derive from the nature and the components of the service situation a basis for the practitioner's account-ability for the foreseeable results of his actions.

Pepper's (1961) discussion of the "contextualistic root metaphor" suggests an approach that is especially relevant to the one recommended here, provided one feels free to equate the social work service situation with what Pepper labels "the historic event." His label may not be too unrea-sonable because he describes the historic event as "the event in its actuality" or, due caution being admonished, an "act."

> When we come to contextualism, we pass from an analytical into a synthetic type of theory. It is characteristic of the synthetic theories that their root metaphors cannot satisfac-torily be denoted even to a first approximation by well-known common-sense concepts such as similarity, the artifact, or the machine. The best term out of common sense to suggest the point of origin of contextualism is probably the historic event. And this we shall accordingly call the root metaphor of this theory.
>
> By historic event, however, the contextualist does not mean primarily a past event, one that is, so to speak, dead and has to be exhumed. He means the event alive in its present. What we ordinarily mean by history, he says, is an attempt to *represent* events, to make them in some way alive again. The real historic event, the event in its actuality, is when it is going on *now*, the dynamic dramatic active event. We may call it an "act," if we like, and if we take care of our use of the term. But it is an act conceived as alone or cut off

that we mean; it is an act in and with its setting, an act of its context [p. 232].

Clients who resort to the social worker for help—whether by contract, direct voluntary appeal, or assignment by third parties (e.g., a welfare department)—are acknowledging that they cannot or are not free to help themselves. The client who is in extreme distress may be even less capable of helping himself, at least at the particular moment when the social work service is initiated. To the extent that the social worker possesses special skills and competence, not generally available to others who lack his education, training, and experience, clients have less capacity not only to provide the necessary service for themselves but to judge the timeliness and adequacy of the worker's interventions in their behalf.

This too is part of the reality of the social work service situation that dictates ethical responsibility. Clients need not be completely incapacitated for the social worker to incur a high degree of ethical responsibility, although such a situation would certainly represent an a fortiori case. The client's *relative* incapacity is the basis for defining the social worker's ethical responsibility in any case. However, the client's relative incapacity, joined with his reliance on the social worker for service, becomes a compelling consideration in shaping the worker's standards of ethical conduct.

Social workers have long stressed the psychological effect on social worker as well as client of the giving and taking of help. An understanding of this effect has been described as basic for the social work practitioner. For example, the topic is included, in the content of the knowledge by which "the practice of the social worker is typically guided ["Working definition of social work practice" (p. 6)]."

Virginia Tanner (1965, p. 62), who has been particularly sensitive to the meaning of the social work service situation for public welfare clients, has discussed some of the risks for the client who finds himself in the position of "asking for something." These risks also indicate the need for social work ethics.

The condition of the social work client in many instances when he seeks help or service, and perhaps because he does, was poignantly described by Florence Hollis (1954):

> Almost universally, when a person comes for help with interpersonal problems, he experiences some anxiety. This is because he usually has some awareness that the problem lies partly within himself. . . . Characteristically, he also experiences discomfort about entering into a dependent relationship. To come for help signifies weakness despite the fact that the recognition of the need for help and the decision to come for it requires strength. One is acknowledging that another is wiser or stronger and taking the first step in allowing oneself to come under the influence of another unknown or little known person [pp. 149–150; see also, Studt, 1954].

And quite obviously, as Gerald Caplan (1961) emphasized, "during the period of upset of a crisis a person is more susceptible to being influenced by others than at times of relative psychologic equilibrium [p. 13]."

The ethical implications of the client's position in relation to the social worker were further underscored by Charlotte Towle (1954):

> A professional person's services are sought because he has a competency, a mastery of knowledge and skill, which the recipient of the service does not have. . . . The practitioner is needed and wanted where there is a problem to solve, when the person is in difficulty, when he may lack his normal adequacy, or may not have the specialized knowledge for the solution of his difficulty. . . . In rendering a professional service constructively, a demand is made that *professional competence shall not undermine the individual, that, in helping him*

> *in the management of his affairs, his capacity for self-management*
> *may not be decreased. Furthermore, respect for the total person . . .*
> *implies that concern for one area of his welfare must not ignore his*
> *general welfare* [p. 4; italics added].

Other human service professions, some engaged in service even less sensitive than that rendered by social workers, are also concerned with such ethical considerations, as demonstrated in the following statement by Edward B. Wilcox (1964), a former president of the American Institute of Certified Public Accountants:

> Wherever anyone performs or offers to perform highly
> skilled and specialized services which are beyond the capaci-
> ties of those who rely on him to judge or measure, he incurs
> an obligation which is professional in nature. In this sense,
> professional men are distinguished, not so much from ama-
> teurs who are not paid, as from merchants or labourers
> whose goods or services can be weighed or measured. This
> kind of professional obligation is a source of prestige to
> those on whom it rests, and it rests on them all the more
> heavily because of this. It is the obligation to render a truly
> sound and useful service in spite of the fact that the profes-
> sional man could probably fail to do so without being caught
> at it. The doctrine of letting the buyer beware cannot apply
> to such service because the buyer must rely on the profes-
> sional attainment and integrity of the person serving him
> rather than on readily measurable results. Quality of profes-
> sional service can be maintained only by the practitioner
> himself, not by his customer or client [p. 1].

If the practitioner's professional obligation is indeed a source of his prestige, his prestige is also a source of his professional obligation. Social work and social workers are not uniformly prestigious, however. Either or both are held in discouragingly low repute in some circles, even among clients. Nevertheless, no matter what the client's view of the social worker is, it represents a realistic component of the social work service situation that implies ethical responsibility. Whether clients regard him with awe or suspicion, the worker is ethically bound to serve them with all the compassion, devotion, and objectivity of which he is supposedly capable. The more undiscriminating the client's view of him is, the more scrupulous he must be with regard to the client's opportunities for and freedom of choice and his own tendency to influence the client unduly. The more hostile the client is to the worker or what he represents, the more cautious the worker must be in his responses to the client. The social worker's aim is to retain his freedom and presence of mind to practice his profession with maximum competence and with maximum regard for the client's welfare and right to service.

The relationship between practitioner and client is rather sacred in social work. Although primarily intended to signify an instrumental but integral medium for the attainment of social work purposes, this relationship has occasionally been described as virtually a functionally autonomous variable in practice. It is sometimes charged with so much sentiment and value that it has all the hallmarks of an independent goal instead of a prerequisite or condition for attaining specific social work service goals.

This apparent accent on the negative is not designed to demean the practitioner-client relationship, although considerable mysticism is still attached to it, but to stress its significance in the social work service situation. That relationship—as the social worker strives to develop it, as the client participates in it, and as it is manifested in social work practice—nurtures some of the most pressing, yet most obscure ethical issues that color the social work service situation. Therefore, it could validly serve as an especially noteworthy determinant of the social worker's ethical responsibility. This applies whether the social worker works with individuals, groups, institutions, or communities, although opportunities for the practitioner-client relationship as well as its nature and appropriateness vary.

What happens at the personal level between worker and client (albeit in the context of the mission in which they are engaged) is fertile ground for unethical conduct by the social worker and hence affords a basis for defining the social worker's ethical responsibility. (This does not mean that clients are "angels"; however, they are the ones for whom service is intended and toward whom social workers owe specific professional responsibility and priority.) To illustrate this point, one can allude to the psychoanalytic phenomenon of transference, which has its counterparts in the relationship between the social worker and his clients, either individually or in groups (e.g., Berg, 1950). The concept of transference is complex, and it has been interpreted, not to mention used in a variety of ways (e.g., Wolstein, 1954). It connotes the client's personal response to the practitioner, which often generates an emotionally derived counterresponse (countertransference) by the practitioner. These mutual responses are not calculated to advance the avowed aims of the service situation, although they may be so utilized.

Whether and how transference should be used in the social work service situation is an issue that involves both competence and ethics. In addition to using deliberate and disciplined responses so that he may apply himself systematically to the professional task at hand, the social worker has the ethical responsibility to avoid exploiting the client's emotional response for his own purposes. If he does not judiciously avoid doing so, he fails in his professional responsibility.

The various transactions between social worker and client—whether they affect the application of eligibility standards, the client's access to particular resources, the worker's reports on his experiences with a client, and so forth—provide another broad basis for defining the worker's ethical responsibility. Such transactions constitute the practical substance of the exchange and negotiations between worker and client and between worker and others in relation to or in matters affecting the client. To develop guides for the worker's ethical conduct, the normative aspects of these transactions must be factored out and understood from an ethical point of view.

Thus if a client is expected to reveal himself to obtain the social worker's service—a demand of the social work service situation, not the invention of clients—the worker is obliged to maintain confidentiality. In this context, confidentiality becomes not merely a sacrosanct value or a right in se but a practical function and consequence of the social work service situation. Some action choices in current practice, which deprive clients of the privilege of confidentiality, are made more easily than they would be if based on the requirements of the social work service situation. Sharing clients' secrets, even within agency administrations, may not be as valid as it seems. Although justified as being in the interest of service to clients, it may not be readily justified from the clients' point of view.

Confidentiality, the responsibility to keep within the relationship between social worker and client the secrets and confidences that the client shares with the social worker, is an ethical and at times a legal duty that is enforced to protect the client in view of the position he is placed in by his need for and recourse to the social worker's service. The sharing of the secrets and confidences, on the other hand, and the assurance that they will remain confidential are necessary for the very performance of the service.

Thus the relationship between social worker and client gives rise to the duty of confidentiality, and the duty of confidentiality in turn gives rise to the relationship between social worker and client. Unless the client feels free to speak freely, the social worker cannot be maximally helpful. If the client does not speak freely because he is uncertain about the practitioner or feels otherwise constrained, the social worker's capacity to be helpful to him is severely limited. The social worker will not find out what he may need to know to be helpful to the client, and he will not have the client's confidence, which may be prerequisite to the client's acceptance of the social worker's influence, guidance, authority, or whatever else the social worker may have to offer to help meet the client's need. In short, the client needs the protection of confidentiality to reveal his secrets, and the social worker needs an awareness of these secrets to help the client.[5]

Understanding the social work service situation may be regarded as "a valid form of knowledge [Polanyi, 1963, p. 39]." Through such understanding, one can anticipate and perhaps explain the possible consequences of the call for the social worker's help and his response to it in terms of a form of knowledge. It would then be possible to communicate and analyze these anticipations and explanations for purposes of education, professional socialization, and practice evaluation. Formulations of ethical principles also constitute a valid form of knowledge.

Although individual social workers make specific action choices when they confront and cope with ethical issues that arise during their dealings with clients, these choices should not be idiosyncratic. They should be based on knowledge that can and must continue to be discovered, collected, pooled, and transmitted by the social work pro-

[5]The term privileged communication is used in law to connote information derived by one person from another because of a confidential relationship between them and to emphasize that the right to a waiver of the privilege belongs to the person, i.e., the client, who reveals the information. The obligation may or may not be incurred by law, however; hence the use of the term confidentiality (Richardson, 1955). (See also Group for the Advancement of Psychiatry, 1960; National Conference of Lawyers and Social Workers, 1968; National Social Welfare Assembly, 1958; Regan T. Macartney, 1956; Whitebook, 1945.)

fession through its accredited vehicles of communication and education.

Although he was not discussing professional ethics as such, Polanyi (1963) made the following comment that is pertinent to this discussion:

> Here then is a brief hint in answer to the great question which I had set aside: namely, whether knowledge, admittedly shaped by the knower, can be determined by him as he thinks fit. A passionate search for the correct solution of a task leaves no arbitrary choice open to the seeker. He will have to guess, but he must make the utmost effort to guess right. The sense of a pre-existent task makes the shaping of knowledge a responsible act, free from subjective predilections, and it endows, by the same token, the results of such acts with a claim to universal validity. For when you believe that your discovery reveals a hidden reality, you will expect it to be recognized equally by others. To accept personal knowledge as valid is to accept such claims as justified, even though admitting the limitations imposed by the particular opportunity which enables the human mind to exercise its personal powers. This opportunity is then regarded as the person's calling—the calling which determines his responsibilities [p. 36].

The practice of social work inevitably entails conflicts of interest between social worker and client, client and client, client and interested third parties, client and agencies, social worker and social worker, clients and society, and so on. Such issues arise constantly, and as a result the social worker is pressed to declare himself in words or deeds. Some of the choices he must make are difficult because too often they are not clear-cut. Thus the outcome can only reflect an assigned priority, based on the social worker's ranking of various levels of professional responsibility in relation to differential obligations to others and perhaps himself as well. Although the answers may be different for different social workers, it may be possible to generalize the *principles* of choice. The key to such a generalization lies not only in the ethical metaphors to which the entire social work profession subscribes but in the social work service situation as each social worker experiences it.

Chapter 5

SOCIAL WORKER AS FIDUCIARY

The nature of social work, the consequences of its status—at least as perceived by persons in need—and the context of its practice make evident the importance of a system of ethics to guide and restrain the social worker. The social worker's occupational responsibility and his occupational opportunity, both deriving from some form of community sanction and both based on assumed competence and the quest of clients for its promised benefits, generate the social worker's ethical responsibility.

For all clients, social work is benevolent work, and for most clients it is also charitable work. Very often no fees are paid to the social worker, and when they are, they are modest or scaled to the client's capacity to pay them, if indeed he has any capacity at all. Most often the social worker's monetary reward is a flat salary: for example, when he administers an agency, works with boards and committees, or works in a public welfare department. His success is not generally measured, either by himself or his clients, by what he accomplishes in his clients' behalf (compare Levy, 1974b). Instead, it is evaluated on the basis of the way he goes about his work: his relationships with others, his skill in dealing with them, how he makes them feel, and so on.

When the social worker's job description includes fund raising, his effectiveness is appraised in relation to the amount of money raised, but even then a premium is placed on his relationships with individuals, groups, and organizations and his capacity for organizing them, helping them to work with one another, and inspiring them to assume increasing responsibility. Furthermore, the social worker who is a fund raiser rarely carries that function exclusively. He also generally carries responsibility for administration, planning, community relations, and the like (Levy, 1973a).

Even the social worker who engages exclusively in the private practice of social work in his own office and receives fees for service directly from his clients is not evaluated on the basis of measurable results—at least not by his clients.[1] If anything, the private practitioner's service is more intangible than that rendered in institutional settings, particularly those settings that are devoted to income

[1]Whether the private practice of social work is appropriate is still a subject of great debate among social workers, although increasing numbers of them are engaged in it, at least on a part-time basis. Those opposed to private practice would require an institutional framework for social work practice—a social agency, for example. Those who support the concept of private practice insist on it as a reflection of true professional status in that, as in law and medicine, it is a practice which practitioners should become equipped enough to carry out independently without accountability to supervisors and administrators and with greater reliance on their own competence and ethics. Obviously, this only accentuates the need for a system of social work ethics—a need that remains no matter how the issue of private practice is resolved. (See Babcock, 1953; Barkan, 1973; M. Cohen, 1966; Drucker & King, 1973; Epstein, 1973; Golton, 1971; Levenstein, 1964).

maintenance, health care, shelter, and other concrete services. The fees paid to the social worker in private practice are certainly not seen, either by client or social worker, as quid pro quos for services rendered.

Whatever the form of payment for the social worker's service; whatever the amount; whoever pays it; and whoever receives it, whether privately or institutionally, the service is regarded as precious and priceless and one that cannot be exchanged for cash. Payment for it, by fee or salary, cannot be viewed as a reciprocal gesture but rather as a kind of practical arrangement, not contingent upon the client's means or financial capacity. The service is obligatory, even for private practitioners, without regard to the actual cost of rendering it.

The service required by the client is a "whole" service, not equatable with the mathematics of fee arrangements, not partialized or apportioned according to the time and labor performed or to be performed by the practitioner.[2] There is no reason to believe that a social worker is freer than the lawyer is to withdraw his service for reasons related "to the amount or timeliness of his fee," rather than for "reasons entirely connected with the interests of his client [Opinion No. 626, 1956, p. 359]," for although the stakes of lawyers' and social workers' clients differ, they range just as broadly for each, and they are just as likely to reach comparable intensities in both. Because, like the law, social work is not a mere "money-getting" trade, the collection of fees from clients is not apt to become a paramount issue unless clear fraud or another serious offense is involved, but certainly not because of the client's manifest lack of financial ability to sustain himself through a course of service necessary for meeting his need or solving his

[2]Compare the view of the attorney's service in *Mutter* v. *Burgess et al.*, 1930.

problem, if that can be foretold.[3] At the very least, the social worker would be obliged to effect a referral so that the need for service would not be neglected.[4]

Thus far, the discussion of social work, social worker, and client and the interrelationship among them amounts to a description of a fiduciary relation that is, in effect, the immediate foundation of social work ethics. Thus transposing the relationship between social worker and client to a fiduciary relation not only underscores the need for a system of social work ethics but also induces its substance. The fiduciary relation, in other words, is an ethics-generating concept, and the translation of the social worker-client relationship into a fiduciary relation makes the basis for and content of social work ethics especially evident.

The relationship between social worker and client is demonstrably a fiduciary relation. Again law, and particularly case law, is helpful in indicating as much. Etymologically, the concept of fiduciary derives from the Latin equivalent of the word trust, which becomes a nuclear intent in characterizing a relation or a practitioner as fiduciary. If there has been an emphasis in common parlance

[3]The freedom of an attorney to withdraw from a case has been held to be seriously restricted, usually being limited to "cause," very much related to the client's impairment of the attorney's capacity to represent the client effectively (Opinion No. 90, 1957, pp. 200–201; Opinion No. 250, 1957, p. 502).

[4]A dramatic illustration of what was considered to be practitioners' justified withdrawal from a case and what in modified form could occur in a relationship between social worker and client is given in *Mutter* v. *Burgess et al.* The client had charged his attorneys with having "framed," "crooked," and "double-crossed" him. It was the court's opinion that "in withdrawing . . . [the attorneys] did what any self-respecting lawyer would have done. The relation between lawyer and client is of a confidential and delicate nature. Within ethical limits, the lawyer owes entire devotion to his client's interest. The accusations made by the defendant [i.e., the client] are of the most serious nature . . . [and] utterly false. . . . The conduct of the defendant made it practically impossible for his attorneys to continue the performance of their contract . . . [p. 270]."

on the concern about money or property at risk in a fiduciary relation, it is probably only because of the primacy in the past and in law of money and property as assets to be protected and preserved. As in other service contexts, there is more at stake and more to be valued than money and property in the social work service situation, although money and property may also figure in the social work relationship. There are other things to be lost or preserved through the social work relationship besides money and property, however, and ethics is a significant means for preserving and protecting them and must make provisions for doing so.

Autonomy and privacy are among the things that may be at risk in the social work relationship, but there may be much else that clients value and over which they feel they have but a tenuous hold when they resort to the social worker for help. The fiduciary relation reflects the kind of thing that may be at risk in the social work service situation.

According to *Black's Law Dictionary,* a fiduciary (or confidential) relation is

> one founded on trust or confidence reposed by one person in the integrity of another . . . Relief is granted in all cases in which influence has been acquired and abused, in which confidence has been reposed and betrayed. The origin of the confidence and the source of the influence are immaterial [p. 775].

The origin of the confidence and the social worker's source of influence have proven quite material, however, and help to explain the need for the social worker's caution should the client neglect to exercise it. "Confidence in an unfaithful man in time of trouble is like a broken tooth, and a foot out of joint [Prov. 25: 19]." Or as Paul Lowney admonishes in one of his Gleebs (1973, p. 36):

> Your love protects me from everyone.
> Everyone?

Yes.
You're forgetting one person.
Who?
Me.

The relevance of the concept of a fiduciary relation between social worker and client is further accentuated by the following statement:

> The courts have always refrained from attempting to give a definition applicable to all possible cases in which the fiduciary relation might arise. Such relation, however, does embrace every possible situation where confidence is reposed on the one side with resulting superiority of the other. Where the facts reveal that trust is confided in one and accepted by him, the fiduciary relation is created. . . . In Cowee v. Cornell, 75 N.Y. 91, 31 Am. Rep. 428, it was said: "Whenever . . . the relations between the contracting parties appear to be of such a character as to render it certain that they do not deal on terms of equality but that either on the one side from superior knowledge of the matter derived from a fiduciary relation, or from over-mastering influence, or on the other from weakness, dependence, or trust justifiably reposed, unfair advantage in a transaction is rendered probable, the transaction is presumed void, and it is incumbent upon the stronger party to show affirmatively that no deception was practiced, no undue influence was used, and that all was fair, open, voluntary and well understood [*Commercial Merchant's National Bank and Trust Co. et al.* v. *Kloth et al.*, p. 218].

The ethical issue for social workers is, of course, not the nullification of their relationship to their clients but the avoidance of the unfair advantage, deception, or undue influence that the social work service situation makes possible. The reasons are that knowledge and ability alone are not sufficient for the standards of social work practice and that clients also need the protection that social work ethics can insure "from ignorance, inexperience, and unscrupu-

lousness [*People* v. *Alfani,* 1919, p. 673]." The less public
the social work service situation (social workers normally
meet unobserved with clients, except when they work with
groups or in public settings), the greater the need for controls. The ethics incorporated by social workers that serves
as a guide for and a restraint on their conduct is prospec-
tively one of the more effective modes of protection and
control.

For some reason, the potential for ethical misconduct
or negligence on the part of social workers is often not as
evident to observers as it actually is and as compared with
other practitioners. In fact, Chief Justice Stacy went so far
as to compare even doctors and clergymen unfavorably
with lawyers on this score:

> Consider for a moment the duties of a lawyer. He is sought
> as a counselor, and his advice comes home, in its ultimate
> effect, to every man's fireside. Vast interests are committed
> to his care; he is the recipient of unbounded trust and confi-
> dence. He deals with his client's property, his reputation, his
> life, his all.
>
> "No profession," says Mr. Robbins in his American Ad-
> vocacy, 251, "not even that of the doctor or preacher, is as
> intimate in its relationship with people as that of the lawyer.
> To the doctor the patient discloses his physical ailments and
> symptoms, to the preacher the communicant broaches as a
> general rule only those thoughts that commend him in the
> eye of heaven, or those sins of his own for which he is in fear
> of eternal punishment, but to his lawyer he unburdens his
> whole life, his business secrets and difficulties, his family
> relationships and quarrels and the skeletons in his closet. To
> him he often commits the duty of saving his life, of protect-
> ing his good name, of safeguarding his property, or regain-
> ing his liberty. Under such solemn and sacred
> responsibilities, the profession feels that it owes to the peo-
> ple who thus extend to its members such unparalleled confi-
> dence, the duty of maintaining the honor and integrity of
> that profession on a moral plain higher than that of the
> merchant, trader or mechanic [*In re Farmer,* p. 663]."

Well, most social work clients are pretty much have-nots, but many do have some property to lose. And although only infrequently is a social work client's life on the line, many a hospital social worker has been in a position to shorten it or to be insufficiently alert to prevent a client from disposing of it destructively. Neither do many social workers have much influence with God, though they could inflict some damage on clients whose problem may be that they are suffering religious guilt or guilt about religion. For the rest, Justice Stacey and his friend Robbins could have been talking about social workers and their clients, even to the point of identifying the loss of a client's liberty at the hands of a negligent or stiff-necked social worker in a department of probation and parole. The law, at least, is "a jealous mistress" and as such does try to watch its practitioners. The social work client is often not so lucky.

Much of the social worker's ethical duty, like that of the lawyer, may be specifically related to the confidence reposed in him by his client. The social work client, like the lawyer's client, is "entitled to believe" that he is under the "care" of the practitioner (*In re Soale*, p. 1069). And as often as not, the social work client is genuinely in need of that "care," whatever the appearance of his need to outside and impartial observers. To the client the need may be realistically and psychologically significant, and that is what he may be entrusting to the social worker along with himself.

The generic consideration that serves as an index to a fiduciary relation is trust and confidence, and perhaps dependence, which the relationship between social worker and client as well as its antecedents generates. This consideration has been a key to the distinction among occupations in case law and offers a key to understanding the need for and nature of social work ethics. A major test, therefore, is whether the service, of its very nature, creates a relationship of trust and confidence. Both in the case of the physician and the lawyer [and on the basis of the discussion so far, one may add the social worker], the person seeking his services must break down the barriers of reserve which otherwise serve to protect him and deliberately reveal to his professional adviser secrets of physical or mental disability, or secrets of business of the most intimate nature. These necessary disclosures create the personal relationship which cannot exist between the patient or client and a profit-seeking corporation. The universal recognition of this immediate, unbroken, and confidential association . . . justifies the rule that . . . allegiance must be wholeheartedly to the patient or the client, and not to another [*Silver* v. *Lansburgh and Bro. et al.*, pp. 519–520].

One problem encountered when contending with the fiduciary relation is the looseness of usage with respect to the terms associated with it: trust, confidence, loyalty, fidelity, reliance, and so on. Horsburgh (1961) is probably justified in insisting that these terms must be distinguished if one is to understand the "dilemmas of trust" and in characterizing trust as a "slippery word in more ways than one [p. 28]."

Although confidence and reliance may lead to trust, at least the trust that can be said to inhere in the fiduciary relation, the question must be raised whether they are a precondition of trust or a consequence of it. Trust may well exist as a kind of residual choice, independently of confidence and reliance. A client may be trusting only because he has no other choice. In that event, does his trust emanate from his reliance and confidence, or are his reliance and confidence a residual consequence of his trust? Or does his trust—because of his lack of options, as is often true when a client resorts to the superior wisdom and skill of a practitioner (as perceived by the client, at any rate) in a realm where, or at a time when the client feels insufficiently competent—dictate his reliance but not necessarily his confidence?

In short, the client needs something about which the practitioner presumably knows something and is able to do something. Short of alternatives, the client entrusts the matter to the social worker, but that hardly means he is confident about the way the social worker will proceed or can truly rely on the social worker. The tenuousness of the client's response only intensifies the need for a deliberate and carefully deliberated system of social work ethics. The social worker, without the constraint of social work ethics, is as likely as other human beings to respond to his client on the basis of whether the client's trust, reliance, and confidence are optional or residual and on the basis of the conditions under which they become manifest. Either way, the client is giving up either choice or jurisdiction. To that extent the client is depending on the social worker's good offices and on his ethics.

Although Erikson (1963, pp. 247–248) wrote in another context, his conception of the word trust (which he prefers to "confidence") makes more evident its ethical implications because "there is more naïveté and more mutuality in it."

The client's relinquishment of control over his own fate in some respect, which is implied in the concept of trust and is operative in the fiduciary relation, is not entirely a function of his own status and power outside the social work service situation. As much as White and Lindt (1963) demonstrate that the behavior of the practitioner (in this case, the physician) is indeed affected by the normal standing of the client, their findings do not gainsay and to an extent support the assumption that the client is moved to "trust" the practitioner. If this is true of the prominent client and peer of the practitioner, who therefore is presumed to know something about what is being done to him, it is bound to be true of the client who ranks low in the social hierarchy; and even of the ranking client to whom the practitioner's practice is essentially a mystery and for whom the need to which that practice is to be addressed is as compelling as it would be to the most nondescript nonentity.

White and Lindt acknowledge the tempering effect on the practitioner when he finds himself treating his colleagues, but they also acknowledge the effect on the client, whoever he is, when he seeks a practitioner's help because "a general of the army or the president of the country, subordinates himself to 'doctor's orders,' and leaves his rank at the hospital door, when he enters it as a patient [p. 304]." In fact, the physician-patient "sometimes throws himself into the role of the patient with a vengeance, being more helpless, more complaining, more apprehensive, and more symptom-ridden than seems justified to those who are taking care of him [p. 305]." This but confirms the observations made by sociologists (e.g., Parsons, 1951; Parsons & Fox, 1952) concerning the trust inherent in the "patient-role," which is as typical of the social worker-client relationship as it is of fiduciary relations in general.

The trusting inclination that characterizes the fiduciary relation and compels the formulation and enforcement of social work ethics is virtually institutionalized and reinforced. Practitioners reward it. A client is "good" if he leaves things to the practitioner (unless, of course, the practitioner values a spark of rebellion and ego-preservation). The "good" client is one who suffers quietly through a painful course of treatment or brutal confrontation.

When Adams and Berman (1965) asked hospitalized children what mother meant "when she tells you at home to 'be good,' " a number of them said: "To help her and do what she says." When asked "What does the nurse mean when she says the child is a good boy or good girl?" a number answered: "To do what the nurse says [pp. 102–104]." And even a five-star general and former president earned kudos for behavior that was not very different (one might say "equally childlike," which after all is in the nature of "trust"): John Eisenhower, during a television interview (NBC-TV, November 10, 1965) in which he discussed his illustrious father's illness and hospitalization, said (approximately): "One of my father's best traits as a patient is that he puts himself entirely into the doctor's hands."

The words vary but the idea is quite consistently expressed—and it applies to the social worker-client relationship: it adds up to a fiduciary relation wherein the client places his trust or confidence or both in the practitioner's integrity and fidelity (also etymologically associated with fiduciary). The trust and confidence are emotionally charged to a degree that is proportionate to the urgency of the client's need, his own condition as a person, and his perception of the practitioner's authority with regard to meeting his need.

> Social objectives clearly depend for their realization upon the existence of a certain amount of mutual trust between individuals or groups of individuals. This suggests that trust is good. But few think that it is. More commonly it is held to be good only when it forms part of a larger whole which includes the trustworthiness of those in whom it is reposed. In the absence of such trustworthiness it simply enables wrongdoers to increase the damage which they do to the community. Trust should therefore be proportioned to trustworthiness, people or groups of people being trusted more or less according to the degree of trustworthiness which they have attained [Horsburgh, 1961, p. 28].

Horsburgh is not talking about social workers and clients, but he might as well be, for an implication of the fiduciary relation that has been said to describe the relationship between social worker and client is the trustworthiness of the social worker. Ethics, in turn, is an index of trustworthiness. There is nothing wrong with a client's trust in the social worker if the social worker is trustworthy. An ethical social worker is trustworthy.

The social worker is a strategically placed participant in the fiduciary relation. The client's trust has as its counterpart the social worker's power, which is in fact a function of that trust. This power is at once a potential instrument in the service of the client and a potential weapon against him. Which it is or will be depends on what the social worker does with it. The use of this power becomes as much of a responsibility for the social worker as the service that the social worker is obliged to provide. In this respect, the worker is a "confronted" person in the sense in which Soloveitchick (1964) has employed the concept.

Thus aside from the conventional pressure on the social worker to live a normative existence, as a social worker he is confronted with imperatives that attach to his relationship to his client, and these imperatives derive from the fiduciary character of this relationship.

The social worker (not unlike other human service practitioners) is therefore faced with the pressure to perform competently his service function and fulfill ethically his commitments as a fiduciary. Lacking sufficient internal pressure, he will require external pressure. Ethics must therefore become a group function if it does not succeed as an individual one. At best it is a collaborative venture between social worker and his peers.

Something is obviously working already. The purpose of social work ethics is to make social work, work better, but it is working reasonably well because of natural social forces and individual intuitions and inclinations:

> Our modern life is based to a much larger extent than is usually realized upon the faith in the honesty of the other. . . . We base our gravest decisions on a complex system of conceptions most of which presuppose the confidence that

we will not be betrayed. . . . Modern life is a 'credit' economy in a much broader than a strictly economic sense [Wolff, p. 313].

What the social worker needs as fiduciary is to make intentional that which is sometimes intuitive since social work responsibility requires deliberateness of action and clarity of purpose in both its practice and its ethics.

Chapter 6

THE POWER BASE OF SOCIAL WORK ETHICS

"Power," as Redlich (1973) said in another but not entirely unrelated connection, "seems the fulcrum of the unethical act [p. 318]." And the relative positions of social worker and client in the social work service situation do effect for the social worker considerable power over the client.

Despite the creation of the National Welfare Rights Organization and various other client and consumer groups (which presumably have represented the interests of clients), the social worker still has the upper hand to a considerable extent. Even a clientele such as the board of a social agency, which has the right to hire and fire the social worker, leaves much to the social worker, if only for its own convenience at the very least and as a manifestation of its confidence in the social worker at most. But whatever the constraints on the social worker's power in his relationship with an agency board, in relation to the agency's clientele the social worker retains and has access to power. For example, a social worker who was an administrator of a home for the aged said, when asked whether the agency's clients were vulnerable to abuse or exploitation:

> Most definitely! We handle their medical, financial, social and physical resources and needs. Most are entirely dependent on us. . . . Oh yes! More and more they rely on my opinion, my decisions. They lose touch with the world, it seems, and depend on my current knowledge. . . . It's a bit of a vicious circle—probably repetitive. . . . It seems that you really can and do help these people—until you gain their confidence. But when you have their confidence, their vulnerability increases.

The social worker's power is a function of the client's vulnerability, and the client's vulnerability is a function of the social worker's power.

J. M. Brown (1964) has defined power in its most general sense as "the ability to produce a certain occurrence [p. 524]" and as the influence exerted by a person or group, through whatever means, over the conduct of others in intended ways. However, he does distinguish between the *capacity* to influence others and the *actual* exertion of influence, admitting nevertheless that ordinary usage does not make a sharp distinction between power and influence. Other scholars do not make a sharp distinction either, although the difference between power in actual use and power in the form of influence or in a form otherwise available for use is generally acknowledged. To contend with the ethical implications of the social worker's power, it is enough to acknowledge that he has it to use and that it can be used ethically or unethically. Here too it has potential for good as well as evil, and often it is up to the social worker to determine which it will be. This alone is a measure of the social worker's power because it is the social worker who has jurisdiction over it, give or take a semblance of resistance on the client's part. As likely as not, the client's resistance will incur the social worker's disapproval as an impediment to social work service, which only serves to reinforce the social worker's point. After all, the client's resistance is but a defense against the social worker's power.

Nor is it entirely valid to minimize the social worker's power by comparing it with political power. In characterizing power as "a creature of habits, of culture patterns woven deeply in the lives of men," Charles E. Merriam (1950) insisted on

> the truth . . . that only confusion will be created by trying to draw too sharp and exclusive a line between political and all other forms of organization. . . . A clearer view is gained by frankly recognizing the fundamental similarity between them, and the parallelism and even frequent interchangeability of function [pp. 8–9].

The pertinence of this statement and its relevance to social work are reflected in other conceptualizations of power. Benoit-Smullyan (1944), for example, defines power as "the capacity to make (or participate in) decisions which require other individuals to act in ways in which they would not act in the absence of such decisions [p. 156]." Max Weber (Parsons, 1947), on the other hand, stresses "the probability that one actor within a social relationship will be in a position to carry out his own will despite resistance [p. 152]."

Though Diesing (1962, pp. 181–182) discusses power in relation to authority in decision-making structures, he accentuates the negative in describing it as the ability to inflict, at will, unpleasant consequences on others. In doing so, however, he illuminates the ethical implications of power, for the capacity to do harm arises out of the authority of the statements and actions of one who is viewed as having the capacity to make affirmative contributions to those affected by them. The concern of those affected, lest the actor cease making the valuable contributions he is perceived to be capable of, determines the extent of his opportunity to inflict unpleasant consequences on them.

Floyd Hunter (1953, pp. 244–245) does find social agency "professionals" to be weak and "marginal" in relation to the community power structure, but that is only in the context of *community* decision-making. They may not be among the "movers" of other men when community decisions are made, but they are power figures in the settings in which they perform their service functions. They may not make the community's big decisions, which affect large masses of persons and local social structures and institutions, but they do influence the big decisions of individuals, including clients and subordinates, among whom may be institutional and community decision-makers.

Ideally speaking—at least from the viewpoint of rendering social work service—social workers influence the behavior of others while fulfilling the *latter's* intentions. The important connotation of power from an ethical point of view, as Goldhamer and Shils (1939, p. 171) emphasized, is the extent to which the social worker influences the behavior of others to fulfill *his own* intentions.

Not all identifiable forms of power are equally evident or even possible in social work practice. For example, Goldhamer and Shils distinguish three forms of power according to the type of influence that is actually or potentially perpetrated on the subordinated persons: namely, force, which involves physical control; domination, which involves explicit commands; and manipulation, which involves subtle or implicit demands [pp. 171–172].

Only manipulation would appear to figure to any appreciable extent in social work practice, certainly in prospect. But that is not entirely true because social work clients in many settings are subject to control by force and domination as well as manipulation. These need not be egregious in their actual operation, but they are often present nonetheless. Clients themselves may collaborate, but they may also lack sufficient autonomy or will even to do that much, which makes them all the more vulnerable to all the forms of power. The encouragement that clients lack as a result of communal or institutional sanction of the social worker's power (which serves to legitimate it) clients may find in their own need, incompetence, despair, or passivity. "Whenever there is acute danger, the impulse of most people is to seek out authority and submit to it [Russell, 1938, p. 19]." Social work clients are often so apprehensive of the danger they face—the danger that propels them toward service or subjects them to it when they are involuntary clients—that they are all too prone to submit to the authority the social worker in fact has or is perceived by clients to have.

Whether physical, verbal, or implicit, power is control when it is both position and action.[1] To control is to exercise power, not simply to have it (National Resources Committee, 1953, p. 667).

The notion of "fate" and "behavior" control, as articulated by Thibaut and Kelley (1959), is an apt description of the kind of power that is most likely to be operative in the social worker-client relationship.

> If two persons interact, the pattern of outcomes given in their interaction matrix indicates that each person has the possibility of affecting the other's reward-cost positions and, thereby, of influencing or controlling him. . . . In other words, the matrix reveals that each person has certain possibilities for exercising power over the other . . . If, by varying his behavior, A can affect B's outcomes *regardless of what B does*, A has *fate control* over B. . . . The larger the range of

[1] "Control means power. Behavior control means power over people. . . . The moral problem of behavioral control is the problem of how to use power justly. . . . All good people who have power over others, even just a little power and even for just a little while, need access to an ethic that can guide their use of it [London, 1971, pp. 250–252]."

> outcome values through which A can move B, the greater his
> fate control over B [pp. 100, 102].

In the social worker-client relationship, the opportunity for
fate control is generally skewed in the social worker's favor.
The same is true of behavior control.

> A second kind of power is called *behavior control.* If by varying
> his behavior, A can make it desirable for B to vary his behav-
> ior, too, then A has behavior control over B. (We use "con-
> trol" here in the sense of ability to affect the likelihood of
> occurrence of one or more behaviors.) . . . The amount of
> this behavior control will depend upon the values to B of the
> various outcomes. . . . B's outcomes vary not as a function
> either of A's behavioral choices (fate control) or of his own
> but as a function of the interaction between them [pp. 103–
> 104].

Since Thibaut and Kelley are dealing with interpersonal relations generally, they naturally emphasize the correlation between A's behavior control and B's adjustment
of his behavior to coincide with A's behavioral choices in
accordance with what B stands to gain through such an
adjustment. However, what B sees as a gain in the social
worker-client relationship may not be objectively valid at
all. It is but gain, as the client perceives it, and how the
client perceives it depends on how the client views the
social worker and what the worker represents in the relationship between them.

The social worker's "affective neutrality," through
which he can remain detached and insulated in his relationship with his client (Blau & Scott, 1962, p. 61; see also
Wilensky & Lebaux, 1958, pp. 298–303), while presumably
functional for social work service, also facilitates the operation of a "law of personal exploitation" since the one who
cares less can exploit the one who cares more. (Thibaut &
Kelley, 1959, pp. 104–110; compare Blau, 1964).

The client has more invested in the outcome of the

social worker's service than the social worker does, and he is more deeply involved in and affected by the quest for it. The client usually depends more on the social worker than the social worker depends on him. That becomes a root of the social worker's power.

> What is dependency? It is an attitude between two persons in which the first one demands or solicits protection or help, or wants the other to take over responsibilities, or delegates to the other person executive functions which he cannot execute for himself. This may be temporary in crises, or a permanent arrangement by the ego. To what is this attitude a response? To an anxiety, which is the emotion that accompanies a state of helplessness. What activities does dependency motivate? To be near the object, to do whatever the object demands in return for the protection or aid, even if this means the surrender of important gratifications [Kardiner, 1937, p. 188; cf. Allen, 1937, pp. 859–869].

The social worker is usually in the position to legislate the rules governing the social worker-client relationship. This is in fact the social worker's responsibility since the client necessarily relies on the worker's competence for the help or service he needs. If the process of acquiring the help or service is not to be completely aimless, the social worker will have to give it some direction. Even though the social worker acknowledges the decision-making jursidiction of the client, he generally monitors the roles that he and the client play in shaping the foundation for the client's choice—if only to avoid the client's irresponsible or passive delegation of responsibility for it to the social worker or to discourage the client's ill-considered conclusion. This responsibility to stage their roles can be carried in a variety of ways, some more strategically designed than others to preempt ultimate control over the client. Nor are clients always unwilling to be controlled. And when they are, the social worker has access to many indirect forms of control that exceed those functional forms which are presumably designed only to improve or facilitate social work service. Even coercion is not always apparent to the naked eye, least of all to the client's, as Breggin (1964) suggested:

> By coercion is meant any action, or threat of action which compels the patient to behave in a manner inconsistent with his own wishes. The compelling aspect can be direct physical or chemical restraint, or it can be indirect threatened recriminations or indirect "force of authority" which convinces the patient that no other legal or medical alternative is available to him.
>
> Coercive behavior falls into the general category of manipulative behavior, in which one person feels that his own actions are determined by someone else, despite his own wishes. Coercion may be considered the experience of an unusually constraining or intimidating alternative, so that the individual feels his freedom of choice is preempted [p. 173].

One hazard to which the social worker's power subjects the client is the "quest for omnipotence" (Sharaf & Levinson, 1964), which feeds on the social worker's good intentions and wanders into the "enforcement of welfare" (Grygier, 1965; Grygier, undated) rather than its nourishment.

Taylor (1958) has confirmed as much with specific reference to social casework. Discussing persuasive control through which individuals are *induced* to conform to the expectations and wishes of others, Taylor points out that every social agency tends to be "normative, evaluative, and judgmental." He identifies verbs such as mold, restore, shape, better, improve, help, encourage, assert, develop, relieve, solve, and resolve, which recur in statements of agency purposes and reflect the tendency to control clients. These words, he says, make it difficult for him to determine where "persuasion stops and coercion begins." He describes "the power element in casework" as follows:

> The counselor may appear to the client as a fount of wisdom or as a storehouse of knowledge and helpfulness which may be given to, or withheld from, the client. Implicit, therefore, in the counselor-client relationship is the presence of power which induces the client to modify his behavior, since he requires what the counselor has to give. The client, overwhelmed by his problem and his feelings of inadequacy in meeting it, imputes power to the counselor . . . Whether or not the counselor wants to be a "power person" in the counseling relationship, he *is* by client imputation [p. 18].

Whether imputed or actual, power is not inevitably used by a social worker in his own self-interest. When it is intentionally used in the client's interest, the social worker is apt to proceed with a self-righteous lack of restraint. Whatever the resulting benefit, which might well satisfy the client, if it is at the involuntary expense of the client's personal control, it represents an abuse of power. In short, the operation can be regarded as a practice success but an ethical failure.

Schorr (1964) has scrutinized the "prescriptive" features of service that permit the social worker to tell a client what to do and thus simply substitute one pressure for another in the life of a harried client. Ginsburg (1963) was equally critical of the concept of "adjustment" as an instrument for molding individuals in the molder's image rather than permitting them to grow to the form and substance to which they have both the right and capacity to grow. Both authors, in effect, caution against the abuse of power and in so doing acknowledge the existence of the power.

One reason for the emphasis on the social worker's power, aside from the possibility of its abuse and therefore its ethical implications, is the nagging possibility that some individuals might very well gravitate toward the practice of social work because of the power it promises, if only for implementing what they envisage as benevolent purposes.

Drawing on Szondi's concept of operotropism, Ilan

(1963) has done an intriguing—almost hair-raising—analysis of vocational choices and the psychological conflicts that motivate them. If similar dynamics operate in the choice of social work, they are likely to materialize in the social worker's power, notwithstanding the following, rather optimistic view of the social worker:

> The social worker while remaining human and sensitive to the infinite nuances of responsive human relationship, is so disciplined in his role that his own personal biases and prejudices are prevented from interfering or intruding into the relationship except insofar as they reflect professional and agency social values [Hofstein, 1964, p. 42].

Hopefully, social workers do ultimately attain this degree of self-discipline. But since there is insufficient assurance that many will, ethics may have to be prescribed, which, if not completely incorporated by all social workers, may serve as corrective or restraining influences on the thirst for and abuse of power over clients. Good will may not be enough. Good education may not be enough. And time itself may be a luxury. In the meantime, a few guides, a number of rules, and a modicum of regulation may have to serve because it may be some time before rank-and-file social workers manage the responsibility by themselves. As the surgeon says in Arthur Miller's *The Price:*

> The time comes when you realize that you haven't merely been specializing in something—something has been specializing in you. You become a kind of instrument, an instrument that cuts money out of people. And it finally makes you stupid. Power can do that. You get to think that because you can frighten people they love you. Even that you love them [p. 54].

Chapter 7

THE RELEVANCE (OR IRRELEVANCE) OF THE CONSEQUENCES OF SOCIAL WORK PRACTICE TO SOCIAL WORK ETHICS

Social work ethics represents behavioral expectations or preferences that are associated with social work responsibility.[1] It is the behavioral dimension of values that social workers consensually adopt, either by formal action of their professional associations or by informal cumulative approval of actions in practice or references in professional literature. On the basis of these values, social workers can decide on or plan their professional moves and evaluate them afterwards. These values can also serve as a basis for regulatory and grievance procedures, designed to encourage ethical social work practice and to adjudicate charges of deviation. Ethics therefore represents preferences, not to the extent that they have *proven* worthy of realization but because they have been *deemed* worthy of realization. These preferences continue to be compiled, modified, and crystallized in response to accumulating knowledge and tech-

[1]This chapter is adapted from Levy (1974).

nology and in response to social change. Despite their
evolving nature, however, they rest on a fairly constant and
fundamental value base with which social workers have
been identified since the advent of their professionalization: that is, from the time that the practice of social work
ceased to be an exclusively voluntary enterprise and
became a full-time, paid occupation, one for which special
preparation became essential.[2]

The value dimension of social work behavior expectations poses different issues than those posed by the practice
dimension of social work, although values do affect social
work practice. The capacity for living up to the requisites
of social work practice is attested to in the answers to ques-
tons such as the following: Can the social worker do what
he is required to in fulfilling social work responsibility?
Does he have the talent and the temperament for doing it?
Does he know how to do it? Does he have aptitudinal and
attitudinal access to the means most suitable for doing it?
Is he aware of and can he employ the most effective approaches for doing the job well in each case, whatever the
nature of the particular social work job and whatever the
level at which it is carried: clinical or administrative, direct
or supervisory? The answers to each of these questions are
factually founded. The social worker either has or does not
have what is required to fulfill the mission of his position
in the light of the best data and techniques available.

The ethics of social work practice, on the other hand,
is attested to in answers to questions such as these: Can or
does the social worker do what is *right* under the circumstances, even when it may not be what is *best* for the purposes to be served by his position? In other words, the

[2]For a graphic illustration of the origins and development of this trend
and for extensive bibliographical and other sources that attest to its
representativeness, see Kusmer (1973).

question is not whether he is *effective* in what he does, but whether he is responsive to all the obligations implicit in his position, normative to it, and held dear by all concerned with it, including the affected parties and others who share a concern for them. Is what he does consistent with the values espoused by social workers collectively, regardless of what he might consider most practical and effective to do in relation to his client's need or problem? Social workers are assumed, by virtue of their office, to "know their job," but they are expected to act in it with a decorum that transcends the requisites of competence.

Principles of social work ethics derive from values that are simply declarations of or that represent a consensus about preferences which may or may not coincide with approaches to the successful fulfillment of professional responsibility. These declarations need not contradict such approaches, but they are not required to coincide with them. They are different orders of things, even though, in professional dicta, goals and prescriptions may each be infused by the other. In fact, professional principles have been sometimes defined as facts infused with values. Social work has been generally defined in such terms in order to make its value and scientific foundations inseparable.

Principles of professional ethics by definition derive from values. Therefore, the anticipated consequences of professional acts cannot serve as a valid basis for formulating principles of social work ethics. The rightness, in ethical terms, of social work acts cannot validly be measured by their practical consequences. The ethics of social work acts must therefore be evaluated separately and differently from the effectiveness of the acts themselves. The ethics of social work acts is not evaluated on the basis of whether the acts "work," that is, whether they contribute to the achievement of a practical, measurable, service end. Rather, it is evaluated on the basis that the acts are congruent with specified values. The acts may indeed "work" (they may be instrumentally effective), but that is not why they are valued or why they may be regarded as ethical.[3]

> [The] straightforward method of answering the questions "Is this the right thing to do?" and "Why ought you to do that?" can apply only to situations to which a rule of action is unambiguously appropriate. The most interesting practical questions, however, always arise in those situations in which one set of facts drives us one way, and another pulls us in the opposite direction. . . .
>
> Given two conflicting claims . . . one has to weigh up, as well as one can, the risks involved in ignoring either, and choose "the lesser of two evils." Appeal to a single current principle, though the primary test of the rightness of an action, cannot therefore be relied on as a universal test; where this fails, we are driven back upon our estimate of the probable consequences. And this is the case, not only where there is a conflict of duties, but also, for instance, in circumstances in which, although no matter of principle is involved, some action of ours can nevertheless meet another's need. . . . We here appeal to *consequences in the absence of a relevant principle, or "duty"* [Toulmin, 1950, pp. 146–148; italics added].

Whether acts in a social work capacity or in fulfillment of social work responsibility are ethical can be determined only by the degree of their compatibility with normative or consensual preferences. The relevant preferences are primarily those of the social work profession, although the profession does incorporate values of the community or society that apply to professional conduct and condition the community's or society's sanctioning of the profession.

The social work profession does concern itself with issues affecting the competence of its members to practice and the proficiency and economy with which they practice. But its ethical concerns, as reflected in its code of ethics and

---

[3]Kleinsasser and Morton (1968) review ethical positions related to "means versus ends (pp. 1–2)."

its procedures for approving or censuring professional acts, derive from values to which it has committed itself and which constitute premises for the professional conduct of its members. These values tend to group themselves as preferred conceptions of people, preferred outcomes for people, and preferred instrumentalities for dealing with people (Levy, 1973e).

Within such categories are included values that represent the consensual preferences of the social work profession. These values will vary in terms of their emotional charge, influence, and enforceability, depending on the extent of the consensus and the intensity with which they are accepted and the significance and scope of their subject matter. As with any other values of any group or society, reactions to professional behavior that disregards or offends social work values will range from mild disappointment to vigorous censure and, in some situations where the law or a form of excommunication applies, deprivation of the right to practice.

Social work as an organized profession has not developed to the point developed by some professions, where the critical reaction of the community of professional peers represents an awesome threat and intimidation. Nevertheless, the norms and preferences of the social work profession, even those about which unanimity has not been attained among social workers, have often been so profoundly incorporated by social workers, especially those socialized by professional education, that they serve as an influential collective superego.[4]

There may be sadness among social workers and despair in the social work profession, but there are no collective sanctions when a particular social work job is not done

[4]"An ethical statement is no longer a report or expression of mores: it is custom transformed into rule, an explicit formalization of the prescriptive customs of the group, deliberately advanced and wielded as a regulative principle [McGee, 1963, p. 202]."

well or effectively, even when there is agreement about what would have made it effective (witness the agony and the futile debate concerning the studies of the so-called effectiveness of social work methods). But if social workers could agree that a professional act is unethical, its perpetrator would also be held to account for it. In short, unethical acts are more readily judged than are unskilled or incompetent ones, presumably because judgments about them are arbitrarily founded. Values are simply enunciated or declared. They are one man's or one profession's preferences as against another's. As such they serve as a major premise against which particular acts may be almost syllogistically appraised.

Although unduly subjective or individualistic for the purpose of this discussion, Haefner's (1961) analysis of the ethical syllogism is applicable to social work ethics:

> By "Ethical Syllogism" we shall understand an arrangement of propositions such that their very structure is a demonstration of how I arrive at, or justify, a judgment of obligation —the feeling, if you please, that "I ought" to do so-and-so, or that "I ought" to act in such-and-such a manner. . . . In the major premise of an ethical syllogism I express *my perception of the social norm* obtaining in such-and-such a situation. In the first minor premise I state my *intention* of accepting the social norm for myself. The conclusion is a judgment of *obligation.* "Then I ought to do so-and-so" or "I ought to behave in such-and-such a manner." This leads to decision and action, or eventually, to justification of an act already done [p. 289].[5]

[5]As some of Haefner's italics and the rest of his discussion suggest, he is addressing himself to individual acts in a general ethical context. Contrary to his intention, his statement is being applied here to social work ethics in the context of social work norms and preferences and is applicable to social workers in general. The acceptance of "the social norm," therefore, is not a matter of individual negotiation and resolution but of an assumed commitment on the part of all social workers. Its application to an individual case, however, is a more individual matter.

To make the point perhaps a bit clearer, one can resort, with only minor adaptations, to Murphy's (1967) analysis of "law logic." If we start with social work values and ethics instead of legal precedents and decisions, as Murphy does, his concept of "law logic" applies to social work ethics.

> The connection between evidence and verdicts, precedents and decisions, is neither inductive nor deductive. . . . The connection between reasons and decisions in the law rests upon the presence of certain conventional rules uniting them. However . . . there is no legal reason to regard these rules as, in any sense, logical. . . . Legal argument employs no special logic and manifests no special pattern or rationality.[6] A legally justified decision is not of necessity a rationally justified decision at all. . . . The rules rendering the conclusion of a legal argument binding are not, like logical rules, rules connecting premises and conclusions at all. Rather they are rules connecting conclusions with *authorities.*[7] The legal rules define, not valid arguments, but valid judicial [social work(?)] behavior [pp. 193–198].

Unethical social work acts, we have said, are more *readily* judged than are unskilled or incompetent ones. They are not more *easily* judged, not so much because of the ambiguity that characterizes values sometimes, but because of the likelihood of myriad minor premises that represent the specific application of values in specific cases. (Practice issues are complex and difficult to judge largely because of

[6]Since Murphy is discussing "law logic," it is a particular logic that is not logical according to the conventions of logic. Similarly, the ethical syllogism is not a conventional syllogism, and conclusions do not follow automatically from the premises. The premises simply provoke judgments that lead to conclusions about justifiable actions or the actions themselves. Analagously, social work ethics represents a special logic of its own, logic sui generis, in which what is accepted is not truths and their interrelationship but duties and obligations as practitioners may apply them to given situations.

[7]In the context of social work ethics, the connection would be between conclusions or actions and the "authority" of social work values.

the multiplicity of causes, variables, and potential instrumentalities for coping with highly variable cases.)

Even when values are unequivocally clear, their applicability to specific cases is subject to scrutiny because of the nature of those cases. Although Begelman (1971) is concerned primarily with the ethics of behavior therapy, critiques of which he takes to task on what he considers to be logical grounds, he does provide a lucid illustration of the issue dealt with here. This illustration is quite pertinent for social work for it deals with the right of a patient to consent to treatment:

> The law does not grant this protection because the patient's wishes are invariably in accord with an independent professional criterion. A patient has a right to decide not because his decision is *informed*, but because his decision is *his* [citing D. B. Dobbs].
>
> The dignitary right of general medical patients to determine what shall be done with their own bodies was enunciated by Justice Cardozo in 1944.[8] Correspondingly, issues concerning the right of the "mental patient" to refuse treatment based on forms of biological or behavioral therapies

[8]The pervasiveness and the reaches of the value on which this right of patients is based were dramatically underscored by Bonhoeffer (1964), who was of course responding to the extreme case of fascistic treatment of human beings: "We speak of exploitation of the human body in cases where a man's bodily forces are made the unrestricted property of another man or of an institution. We call this state of affairs slavery. But this does not refer simply to the system of slavery in antiquity. There have been historical forms of slavery which have preserved the essential liberty of man more effectively than do certain social systems in which the concept of slavery is itself rejected but the men who are said to be free are in fact totally enslaved. . . . [Slavery] exists wherever a man has become exclusively a means to another man's end [p. 184]." The subjection of patients or clients to procedures against their will or without even testing for it, even "for their own good," would offend this value, especially if some institutional, educational, or professional interest is given precedence over the patient's or client's jurisdiction over his body or being. This is often an issue in social work practice.

may emanate from similar extensions of the same legal philosophy. The possibility of the wider applicability of these legal principles implies that the documented efficacy of a treatment approach does not define all the ethical requirements germane to administering it in particular cases.

In spite of this, there are inherent limitations on the extent to which the patient's free consent to treatment may be an ethical requirement. We do not obtain such consent from children, autistic or otherwise. Here we confer upon the parent jurisdictional rights. When the child has no parents or is a ward of the state, the jurisdiction may be assumed by the therapist himself, with upper administrative clearance. Similarly, we may not require consent to treatment on the part of self-destructive, self-mutilating or nonverbal adult patients. But these exceptions cannot form the basis of generalized repudiation of the requirement of free consent [p. 167].

The consequences of particular social work actions in particular cases do not make for ethical principles. That is, the anticipated or experienced consequences of an act are not the reason for the formulation of an ethical principle nor for the nature of its formulation. The variability that may occur in relation to the ethical principle, more independently formulated on the basis of values held by the members of the profession, occurs in applying it or in the decision not to apply it.

Nevertheless, ethical principles do have consequences that can hardly be ignored, even in an ethical framework. A proposition may be enunciated which is consistent with the idea that anticipated or experienced consequences are not a valid basis for the formulation of ethical principles and yet be realistically cognizant of the impact of consequences.[9] The proposition is the following: The relevance

[9]For empirical confirmation of this position, one need only reverse the order of analysis and derive a value from the consequences of professional acts by considering the choices of professional acts in a variety of case circumstances.

of consequences to the ethics of social work is that when the professional action choice is made on the basis of duty or obligation rather than its efficacy, it is an important part of ethical responsibility to contemplate the consequences of the action, including those that affect values.

The purpose of this proposition is not to establish the ethical principle that is applicable to a case but to consider the operational effects of the principle that is applied. In other words, although consequences do not shape ethical principles (values do that), the anticipation of consequences is a component of ethical responsibility. Before a social worker acts, whether in response to his professional judgment concerning the needs of a case or in response to professional values, he owes his clientele the obligation to contemplate the consequences of his professional acts. The reason for this is that the social worker has the ethical responsibility to make provision for the consequences that his own professional acts may generate and to determine a priority ordering of the alternatives at his disposal and of the values affecting them that may be in conflict with one another. As Wolf (1972) has put it in relation to psycho-analysis, "the analytic position is that it is immoral to be unconscious of the implications and consequences of one's behavior [p. 487]."

A social worker can hardly feel ethical in the line of practice if he persists, even in accordance with an unequiv-ocal value, in engaging in professional acts that devastate a client or a group or deprive one of an option, if not an opportunity. On the other hand, a social worker bent on ethical as well as proficient practice can hardly resort to anticipated consequences as a means for formulating an ethical principle by which his professional conduct will be guided. An illustration in social work practice with groups will suggest the implications of this proposition. At the risk of complication, a case will be cited, the substance of which joins the issue of consequences of the group's actions and the issue of the consequences of the social worker's interventions in the light of the value involved.

The case in point concerns the social worker's role in relation to a group that engages in unethical behavior. Thus an ethical issue is posed for a social worker who confronts an ethical issue. The situation involves a group that steals in the presence of its social worker. Aside from the principles of efficacious practice by which he may be guided, the worker has before him a problem of ethics in the substance of the case and a problem of ethics with respect to the choices of action at his disposal. The consequences of concern to him as a social worker relate to the acts of both the group and himself. If he does nothing, he appears to acquiesce in the offense of stealing, and the group experiences the practical results of the theft.

The worker may approach this issue from the point of view of simply coping with the group to affect its behavior or of dealing with it in a manner that impresses it with its social obligations. He must also approach the issue from the viewpoint of the consequences of his action or inaction. Whatever the implications of his actions in terms of skill and competence, those actions carry ethical connotations to the extent that they respond to or represent certain values. He is thus concerned with two sets of consequences, and why he does or does not do what he does or does not do about them represents his ethical stance, or his activation of ethical principles.

If the social worker is working with a street gang or other group whose values differ from those he represents and he fears their alienation if he upholds values that differ from theirs, his choice of action may be designed only to forestall such alienation. That is a practice choice, but is not addressed to his own ethical responsibility or to a value-based end for the group, and it confuses the ethical issues, even if it clarifies issues related to his relationship to the group. On the other hand, his attention to his relationship with the group may be at the expense of his ethical obligations. He is not contemplating sufficiently the consequences of his acts if he concentrates on his relationship with the group to the exclusion of the values he is supposed to represent as a social worker and the ethical obligation he owes to the group to intervene in their antisocial acts. In other words, in selecting his professional course of action, he is not reckoning with the possible consequence that he will neither be representing a social attitude nor trying to change an antisocial one. In considering the consequences of his action, however, he need not be relying on consequences to shape the ethical principles which guide him but simply considering the consequences in selecting his mode of professional intervention.

The following chart suggests the range of choices at

Chart 7–1

Degree of Reliance on Consequences of Worker's Action as a Premise for Defining Ethical Responsibility

		None	Consideration for others	Personal effect on perpetrator	Matter of perpetrator's negotiation
	Wrong in itself				
Characterization of the Group's Act	Wrong because it deprives another person				
	Not wrong, only risky because one might be caught				
	Not wrong; quite justifiable in view of society's wrongs				

the social worker's disposal with respect to both his own professional acts and the act of the group.

The social worker who contemplates the consequences of his professional acts when determining an ethical course of action for himself, instead of using the probable consequences to formulate the ethical principle to guide his professional actions, considers both the meaning of the group's action to the group and the meaning of his action in relation to the group's action. In the first instance, the group may be afforded an opportunity to consider its act as wrong in itself and, on that ground, worthy of avoidance. Or the group may be influenced to avoid the action only because it deprives another person of property that belongs to him. Or the group may be permitted its inclination to disregard the wrongness of the act, as long as it does not get caught. Or the group may be encouraged in its tendency to regard the act as entirely justifiable in view of the wrongs and deprivations it perceives have been heaped upon it.

The social worker may be guided in his course of action by the inherent wrongness of the act of stealing without regard to the practical effects of his course of action. Or he may importune the group to consider the effects of its act on the victim without reference to the immorality of the act. Or he may caution the group against the act, not because of its wrongness, but because of practical considerations such as having to pay a penalty for it. Or finally, and perhaps extremely, the worker may identify completely with the group in its inclination to steal and in its feeling of justification for that act and simply instruct the group in how to avoid or deal with confrontations with the law.

Without implying an abrupt or arbitrary practice approach, one could account for consequences in a case such as this by anticipating the group's inferences about the worker's values from his choice of intervention and hence arrive at a preferred mode of intervention. The worker can also intervene with reference to the group's existing value orientation in an attempt either to reinforce or to modify it, depending on its nature and proponents. But this again is a matter of ethics and not efficacy; it is related to what it is right for the worker to do, not what is better or more effective. As Begelman (1971) put it (do not lose sight of the context in which he wrote):

> the effectiveness of a technique is not a sufficient condition for whether its application is ethical. Alternatively, the unethical application of any technique may not make it any less effective in bringing about desirable behavior change [p. 168].

It would be reckless disregard of a client or group for a worker, in his zeal to conform to social work values, to ignore negative or destructive consequences for the client or group. It might be unethical practice, on the other hand, for him to ignore social work values entirely only because of anticipated consequences. The ultimate choice of professional intervention must be made more discriminatingly in either case. If a priority ordering must be made between the two, however, the choice would appear to be on the side of ethical principles based on values. When the ethics of a case is clear—although it sometimes is not—the reason for deviating from ethical principles must be clearly compelling. Then, at least, the ultimate choice of intervention can be acknowledged as based on the consideration of valid exceptions rather than substitute principles. The latter is too likely to dilute ethical principles and make them unduly ambiguous.

Undiluted and less ambiguous, on the other hand, ethical principles serve as general guides to ethical social work practice. These principles being established and crystallized, social workers can either apply them to cases as they arise and as appropriate or seek proper validation for exceptions. Then, perhaps, these ethical principles will occasion for social workers in general the kind of introspection and soul-searching that is so imperative to ethical social work practice.

Chapter 8

ETHICS OF PLANNED CHANGE

Social work has been conceptualized as an approach to planned change, or as a "process of giving help to people ... who must change, in order to improve their level of functioning [Lippitt, Watson, & Westley, 1958, p. 4]."[1] This approach has been described as applicable to clients at all levels of social work practice, including clinical and administrative work with individuals, families, groups, organizations, and communities.

The concept of planned change has included not only practice *with* various types of clients toward the end of effecting improvement in their level of functioning, but also direct action *on* the institutions, governments, communities, and societies around clients to effect significant and far-reaching institutional and social changes. When the social worker helps his clients to affect governmental and communal institutions rather than act on them himself, his

[1]This chapter is adapted from Levy (1972c).

94

professional aim is to effect change in his clients so that they, perhaps with his collaboration and facilitation, may make the kinds of changes in the institutions around them that will net for them more of the available rewards, resources, and opportunities.

The social worker who works with welfare recipients illustrates this conjunction of client and institutional change when he strives to effect change in the recipients in order to effect what he regards as desirable changes in the welfare system. Through the social work helping process, the social worker evokes in his clients a revised view of their rights and entitlements, and of their own role in and capacity for realizing them. As the clients change, they use newly acquired capacities and newly inspired will to modify welfare departments and their policies and practices toward the end of accruing more benefits and better treatment for themselves.

The concept of planned change as indicative of social work practice raises many ethical questions. First, it implies certain prerequisites that become the social worker's ethical responsibility. When a social worker is professionally oriented to apply the concept of planned change, he needs a thorough grounding in the nature, process, components, and consequences of personal and social change, both historically and dynamically. To consciously and deliberately use himself as an intervening agency (in this capacity he is often described as a "change agent"), he must understand why, how, and under what circumstances persons, groups, organizations, or institutions change their functioning.[2]

For the social worker, this understanding is similar to

---

[2] "*Planned change* . . . originates in a decision to make a deliberate effort to improve the system and to obtain the help of an outside agent in making this improvement. We call this outside agent a *change agent* [Lippitt, Watson, & Westley, 1958, p. 10]." The "system" alluded to refers to the "client system" or "the specific system—person or group —that is being helped [p. 12]."

his understanding of the growth and behavior of persons, social groups, and institutions in society. He bases his judgments with regard to the action he feels it is his responsibility to take, as well as his ultimate choices of action in relation to those he serves, on this understanding. In addition, since the social worker is but one species of change agent, his professional orientation to planned change requires elements that distinguish his orientation from the professional orientations of other change agents, although not all of the elements of his professional orientation are inevitably distinguishable from those of other professions. These elements certainly need not be mutually exclusive or contradictory. Nevertheless, some differences are indicated if the division of labor among various change-oriented professions is to be determined intelligently.

One basis for differentiation among change agents is the professional functions these agents represent. Both the psychiatrist and the social worker may regard themselves as change agents. Nevertheless, they do represent different professional functions, which would (or should) lead to differences in the specific ends sought through professional intervention, differences in modes of intervention, and differences in knowledge, competencies, and skills relevant to these modes of intervention. There may be a large amount of overlap between psychiatrist and social worker in these respects, but the differences have to be sufficiently significant to reflect the division of professional labor between them and to justify differences of background, education, and training. Some boundaries are necessary to define professions; their functions—as sanctioned by society—their methods, and the knowledge premises on which their functions and methods are founded require some delineation.

Another basis of differentiation among change agents is the value orientations by which they are guided. The social worker's value orientation with respect to planned change ought to be consistent with the social worker's professional function and with the codified values and ethics of the organized social work profession. Such an orientation would suggest ethical guides for professional practice in relation to planned change. The necessary emphasis here is on what social workers value and what bearing their professional values ought to have on their choices of professional actions or strategies of intervention in relation to planned change.

Values being the ideals and preferences of a group toward which its members have an affective regard, one can understand the responses of clients to personal or social change or to the prospect of it—planned or otherwise—on the basis of clients' values in relation to change.[3] Clients at any level of social organization, to which the social worker's professional responsibility happens to correspond, have value predispositions toward or against changing or being changed. These value predispositions constitute an important determinant of the social worker's value orientation as he contemplates planned change. The issue is not the professional skill required but whether the social worker will honor his clients' values and how he will take them into account when selecting courses of professional action that affect his clients. Brief consideration of a few of these value predispositions of clients, which would affect their view of the prospect of planned personal or social change, should attest to their relevance to social work ethics.

Clients often have specific inclinations with regard to change or the prospect of change. They may be highly motivated to change or extremely resistant to doing so. Their responses to the suggestion of or the pressure for

[3]Compare the definition of values in *The Random House Dictionary of the English Language* (unabridged edition), which suggests that values may be either positive or negative—that is, affective regard may be *toward* or *against* an object or prospect, depending on one's values.

change may be psychologically derived. They may dread different ways of coping with their situations and conditions. On the other hand, their responses may be practically motivated. Clients may dread the real consequences of changes they are asked to make in their mode of functioning. A youth who is being guided toward personal emancipation may struggle to remain dependent. A group may prefer to retain its restrictive admissions procedures because its members enjoy the superior status implied by these procedures and thus resist moves toward democratization. A community or society, out of zeal to preserve its history and identity, may block attempts at technological improvement.

Very often these inclinations are culturally reinforced. The charge has been made that in our time and place, change is inherently valued in some circles. For many, what is new or different is ipso facto good. In other circles, change is devalued. Tradition is the guiding motif. In addition to other reasons for welcoming or resisting change, clients have some kind of value predisposition toward the idea of change—for, neutral, or against. The social worker can hardly ignore this predisposition. He must first evaluate his own or his profession's choices with regard to change and his readiness to relinquish his aspiration to effect planned change should his clients prefer not to have it. He must also understand this predisposition if he is to deal with it, even if dealing with it means overcoming value-based resistance to change. In short, such a value predisposition is a practical consideration as well as an ethical consideration for the social worker.

Clients, even those who acknowledge their need for the social worker's service and invite it, may value the option to determine their own course and destiny more highly than the need for change. Conversely, they may prefer to have others make decisions for them (Levy, 1963b). The social worker, in turn, must clarify his own value predispositions in relation to those of his clients. A client's inclination to preserve his own self-determination at all costs, even to the point of resisting the social worker's strategic interventions, is especially difficult for the social worker who is already identified with the value of self-determination. As expressed in the "Standards for the Professional Practice of Social Work" (adopted by the Delegate Assembly of the American Association of Social Workers in 1951), the social worker has "unswerving conviction of the inherent, inalienable right of each human being to choose and achieve his own destiny in the framework of a progressive, yet stable, society [p. 3]."[4] If clients feel justified in resisting the social worker and the prospect of change that he presents, the social worker will have to come to value terms with them, particularly if the planned change he envisages represents a hard imperative for him.

Clients may also differ with the social worker in their interpretation of what constitutes improvement. They resist the idea of change because they do not consider the social worker's planned change as valuable, regardless of his factual data and experience.

Or clients may find their inclinations too precious to subject them to modification. An ethnic group's comfort and security in the selective association of its members with one another, for example, may cause it to repel efforts to get them to include members of other ethnic groups. The rituals of a religious group (a snake sect, for example) may mean too much to it to permit consideration of alternatives, even in the interest of health and life. In each case, the change proposed or intended by the practitioner represents to the client something to be avoided. This feeling exists despite what the practitioner considers the compelling evidence dictating change.

---

[4] The last phrase sounds a bit like the association taketh away what it hath given, but since the only problem is a bit of ambiguity in the context and not in the principle, the value is cited as stated.

The social worker must weigh carefully clients' responses to his role as change agent and to the change that he advocates especially when his clients' estimation of him and his profession is low. He must also carefully explore his own responses to theirs. It is not enough for him simply to overcome his clients' resistances with expertise. He must also decide to what extent he will take into account the values that generate the resistance. Clients who have a cynical view toward social workers' commitments and loyalties may question the workers' good faith in relation to the changes they espouse or promote. Respect for their views may require of the social workers a greater emphasis on a demonstration of their good faith than on their assertion of it and the presumed value of the change they advocate.

The priority ordering of changes by clients on the basis of their value predispositions may not always coincide with that of the social worker. Though his priorities may in fact be more judicious than theirs and be more practically related to what is attainable or is a prerequisite for other changes, the clients may not think so. They may also be right. With this fact, too, the social worker will have to make his value-oriented peace, not simply so he will know what to do, but whether he should do it at all: that is, whether it is ethical to do it.

Although clients may value the prospect of change, they may prefer a different timing. If they are more radically oriented than the social worker, they will seek action "now." If the worker is more radically oriented, he will press for immediate change while the clients hold out for long-range change. Justice and opportunity may be on the clients' side, and the social worker may know it; therefore, he will have to contend with their values. His objective will be to arrive at a course of action that will seem right to him and compatible with the professional values to which he subscribes. In these instances, the social worker's criterion for a choice of action is what he regards as right and good, not what he regards as more efficient or successful, even in terms of the objectively verifiable benefits to be accrued to his clients.

It is also incumbent upon the social worker to crystallize his own value orientation with respect to planned change. Some of his dilemmas in professional practice relate to the congruity or incongruity between his value orientation and those of his clients. Their resolution will depend in great measure on the values by which he is guided in his practice and their correlation with the values that dictate his clients' responses to the personal or social change to which his practice is geared.

A brief consideration of some of the locuses of the social worker's value predispositions in relation to planned change should suggest some of the sources of value conflicts he may have with his clients. It should also show some of the sources of value conflicts he may experience within himself as he selects or discards modes of professional intervention that affect his clients.

The social worker, having taken stock of the internal and external conditions affecting his clients, charges these conditions and his approaches to them with his own affective regard and, on that basis, values change or stability. His valuation of the need for change in his clients' functioning or circumstances may or may not coincide with his clients' valuation. In any case, the social worker's values require scrutiny before as well as when they are applied toward the end of effecting planned change.

The social worker who places a premium on his role as change agent will tend to value change above adaptation and accommodation. He will orient his practice primarily to change, either in his clients' functioning or in the functioning of institutions around them. The queasiness that social workers feel about their clients' "adjustment" may be explained by the social workers' relatively high valuation of change, especially external or environmental change. But they will react similarly to clients' resistance to internal change when they view the clients' own functioning as in need of improvement. In both cases change is valued by the social worker, although a debate among them might be precipitated concerning who or what should do the changing. The social worker's valuation of his role as change agent goes quite far in determining his choices of professional action as well as his experiences in relation to his clients.

Clients' resistance to personal or social change and thus to the social worker's attempts to effect it may be viewed by the social worker as a hindrance, an obstacle, or a nuisance to be surmounted. This resistance can also be viewed as a reflection of values that merit preservation and respect. The substantive merits of the planned change notwithstanding, the accreditation of the clients' resistance on the grounds of self-determination or the sheer strength and identity that the resistance represents would depend on the social worker's affective regard for the clients' response, to the point, perhaps, of laying aside professional goals related to personal or social change.

The social worker may be so intent on attaining goals to which he assigns high priority that he may not look beyond them to the chain of consequences and interactions that they might set off. The effect of planned change on clients—on their lives, their situations, their relationships —merits the social worker's professional concern. This concern is a matter of values as well as rational consideration of the consequences of available alternatives. The degree of responsibility the social worker feels for the aftermath of the change that is stimulated by his professional intervention, as well as for the change itself, becomes an integral part of his value orientation as a change agent and therefore of his ethics as a social worker.

The values of his clients in relation to the personal and social change toward which the social worker has a positive

affective regard ought to discipline his choices of professional action. Similarly, the social worker's values ought to
discipline his action choices with regard to the prospective
consequences of his actions, not only as far as the contem-
plated change is concerned, but also as far as the process
of effecting it is concerned. These constraints shape the
behavioral expression of the values to which he is oriented
—or his ethics.

Social workers share values that represent their preferences with regard to the *ways* of fulfilling professional responsibility as well as the responsibility to fulfill it and to
whom. (See, for example, "Profession of Social Work" and
"Working Definition of Social Work Practice.") It is not
only what the social worker does that constitutes a professional concern but how he does it. The social worker also
owes professional concern for the effect he has on clients
before he does anything, while he is doing it, and after he
has done it. A "good" (i.e., practical) solution to a client's
problem may be discarded or avoided by a social worker if
it is to be applied at the expense of the client's dignity or
autonomy. Although the worker may not discard it, social
work values press in that direction; if they do not press a
social worker firmly enough to influence his behavior, he
may be adjudged unethical.

The emphasis here has been on value considerations
affecting the social worker's role as change agent because
the social worker may regard the need for change at so
many levels of society as so imperative that he can lose sight
of his value-based responsibility toward the clients through
whom, with whom, and for whom his professional efforts at
planned change are intended. Fortunately, the social worker's clients are not the exclusive channel for change, although they are an extremely important one. Other
channels are available to social workers through which necessary changes can be effected. To the extent that clients
themselves are an important or necessary medium and lo-

cus of change, however, the social worker who works with them must not abandon himself to his commendable quest for their personal and social improvement to the point where he abandons his clients and their values, and those values of his own and his profession that assign priority to the integrity, freedom, and will of his clients.

Chapter 9

SOCIAL WORK ETHICS: GENERALLY
SPEAKING

The foregoing has set the stage for social work ethics. The next few chapters discuss the substance of social work ethics. Not that this discussion can be definitive. "Ethics cannot be summed up in a series of inviolate rules or commandments which can be applied everywhere and always without regard to circumstances, thought of consequences, or comprehension of the ends to be attained [MacIver, 1955, p. 120]." At the same time, social work ethics cannot be relegated to the realm of complete and exclusive subjectivity. Although, in the final analysis, ethics represents or affects the action choices of each social worker in the face of ethical issues he confronts in his practice, the premises of these choices are more than his alone to appraise. They must be appraised and anticipated by social workers in general and then, perhaps, serve as guides to the social worker's action choices in specific cases.

Social work ethics thus becomes an agency of social control (cf. Monypenny, 1955), a professional standard by

which individual social workers can be guided as they encounter ethical issues in their practice. Therefore, social
work ethics is aimed at ends that affect clients and others
as classes of persons and at social workers as a class of
persons who affect them. Social work ethics is consequently
not idiosyncratic but normative in effect—or at least that is
what it is intended to be.

Social work ethics in this respect is a system of control
that affects groups of persons and institutions and not
merely isolated individuals. It affects such groups in the
context of transactions shared or experienced by members
of specific groups. Social work ethics must therefore be
formulated in a manner which is empirically realistic—that
is, related to actual experience or to anticipated experience
based on actual experience—and is in accordance with conceptions of what service ought to be like as well as what it
is actually like. Whatever conflicts the social worker perceives when applying formulations of social work ethics, for
him they must be characterized by applicability to social
work service situations. Social work ethics must be serviceable as a guide to professional conduct, which does not
mean that it does not pose innumerable problems.

Montaigne offered some penetrating insight on this
score, although in his time social work could hardly have
been so much as a gleam in his eye:

> Since the ethical laws, which concern the individual duty of
> each man in himself, are so hard to frame, as we see they are,
> it is no wonder if those that govern so many individuals are
> more so [Frame, 1957, p. 819].

And in his ingenious fashion he proceeded in another
essay to validate the continued quest for the formulation of
a system of social work ethics when he wrote:

> As conscience fills us with fear, so also it fills us with assur-
> ance and confidence. And I can say that in many perils I have

walked with a much firmer step by virtue of the secret knowledge I had of my own will and the innocence of my intentions [Frame, 1957, p. 265].

No system of social work ethics could possibly do the
entire job for any social worker. Each social worker will
inevitably have to suffer through the conflicts, implications,
and ambiguities of any ethical issue that he may encounter
and that could not be foretold until he experienced them
—certainly not in the way in which he experiences them.
And yet a sound and carefully thought-out system can at
least serve as a basis for further thoughtful deliberation on
his part and for better-reasoned conclusions. It affords an
approach to the illumination of what T. S. Eliot, in "The
Hollow Men," described as a shadow "between the idea/
And the reality/ Between the motion/ And the act" that
Yarmolinsky (1966) said, with reference to the principal
business of government, makes "it possible for action to
follow thought in orderly sequence [p. 70]." It becomes the
social worker's task, when contemplating his ethical
choices, to, as Yarmolinsky put it, "grapple with the
shadow."

Social work ethics, systematically formulated, alerts
the social worker to those considerations that must be
taken into account before making his final action choices.
Well incorporated by the social worker, social work ethics
makes possible more rapid, but not less well conceived
action choices when time is of the essence in a practice
situation. Vickers (1965) labeled the mental process that
this implies as "appreciation," which he said, apropos of
institutional policy and executive decisions,

> manifests itself in the exercise through time of mutually
> related judgments of reality and value. These appreciative
> judgments reflect the view currently held by those who make
> them of their interests and responsibilities, views largely
> implicit and unconscious which none-the-less condition

> what events and relations they will regard as relevant or
> possibly relevant to them, and whether they will regard
> these as welcome or unwelcome, important or unimportant,
> demanding or not demanding action or concern by them.
> Such judgments disclose what can best be described as a set
> of readinesses to distinguish some aspects of the situation
> rather than others and to classify and value these in this way
> rather than in that [p. 67].

Properly incorporated by the social worker, social
work ethics—to the extent that it can be articulated and
accepted as a valid guide to ethical conduct in its myriad
ramifications in social work practice—can become a
"habit" and hence less and less necessary to negotiate
anew.

> Be quick in carrying out a minor commandment as in the
> case of a major one, and flee from transgression: For one
> good deed leads to another good deed and one transgres-
> sion leads to another transgression; For the reward for a
> good deed is another good deed and the reward for a trans-
> gression is another transgression [*Ethics of the Fathers*].

More specifically, social work ethics serves three essential professional purposes. It is a guide to professional conduct, it is a set of principles that social workers can apply
in the performance of the social work function, and it is a
set of criteria by which social work practice can be evaluated. These are not three definitions of social work ethics;
nor do they imply three types of formulation. On the contrary, the same type of formulation can serve all three purposes because the difference among them is not the mode
of formulation but the time, place, and manner of its application. But social work ethics concerns the value premises
of the social worker's actual or preferred professional conduct rather than the skill or efficiency with which he does
what he does despite the probability or possibility that it
may be evaluated as "good" or "bad."

Particular skills suggest criteria for evaluating the proficiency or outcomes of the social worker's practice, although they may also represent instrumental values—preferences with respect to means for attaining specifiable service ends. Social work ethics, on the other hand, is based on intrinsic values—preferences regarded as right in themselves and as related to what are regarded as the social worker's moral obligations. They are "required," though they may not be demonstrably more proficient than alternative choices.

Social work ethics, as already intimated, affects the substance of the social worker's technical competence as a social worker less than the manner in which that competence is applied in a client's behalf. A modicum of competence must be assumed before ethical issues can be contended with because the ethical component of social work practice implies choice on the social worker's part and the capacity to exercise it. Without a minimum standard of competence, acceptable to social workers as an organized professional group or to some accredited group qualified to judge competence, ethical issues are rather moot, not because practitioners' acts may not be ethical by any standards, but because such acts may not be affirmatively, deliberately, and intentionally so.

Similarly, social work ethics and systems of regulation and evaluation of social workers' ethical conduct require sanctioned practice—that is, practice by qualified and franchised practitioners with acknowledged competence and approval of the right or freedom to practice. The existence or nonexistence of social work competence, as adequately as it may be defined, can itself be conceived of as an ethical issue. An individual who presumes to provide a client with help or service, although he suspects or knows that he lacks at least the minimum competence acknowledged by accredited authority to be prerequisite to the provision of that help or service, and perhaps even lacks the background to judge whether he has such competence, may be considered unethical if he attempts to render that help or service— certainly in a paid or official capacity.

Social work is not the only human service profession to have been concerned about the issue of competence— a fact that can hardly be dismissed, although its relationship to social work ethics must be discriminatingly considered. A symposium on medical education (Stark, 1964), for example, stressed as reasons for continued (not merely initial) medical education, the public's concern about professional competence. The ethical import of the concern did not escape notice, however:

> The physician, who has always enjoyed high status in our society, is now increasingly becoming subject to public evaluation and criticism, much of which has focused around *his role in society* and *his personal relationship* with patients [p. 115; italics added].[1]

Social work associations certainly have been preoccupied with the issue of competence, very much as an ethical concern. The Committee on the Study of Competence of the National Association of Social Workers (1965) listed the following as matters to which it was giving attention:

> 1. The nature and components of competence in social work.
> 2. The ways in which other professions assess competence.
> 3. The methods that could be used to test or assess objectively those elements that are essential to competence.
> 4. The appropriate system for the social work profession to use in the designation of levels of competence [p. 1].

The ethical implication of this concern about competence as such was reflected in the organization's "sense of

---

[1]The transprofessional implications of the observation may be reflected in the fact that the author was an attorney rather than a physician.

urgency" that prompted the request for a study of competence. This urgency was related to the organization's feeling of obligation "in the public interest to define the nature of its competence" and to strengthen and express "with more consistency" certified levels of competence (p. 1).

The committee's published report (National Association of Social Workers, 1972) underscored further the ethical implications of its concern:

> The Committee . . . concluded that the level of competence for *self-regulated professional practice* was the appropriate one for efforts at definition and assessment. . . .
>
> Responsible, self-regulated practice involves the dependable exercise of critical judgment, the ability to make wise decisions and to apply well-developed skills in appropriate action. Essential, too, is the knowledge of when and how to use consultative help. These abilities rest upon the incorporation of professional values, knowledge, and technical skills, as well as the development of professionally directed self-awareness that assures self-direction, voluntary seeking of consultation when necessary and continuous personal effort for improvement of practice. It should be noted that self-regulated practice does not imply freedom from administrative accountability to the agency of employment or, in the case of private practitioners, professional accountability to client systems and the profession [p. iv].[2]

Although the possession of technical competence as such may constitute an ethical issue in this framework, what is particularly germane here is the manner and purpose of its application by the social worker. Moreover, the relative interests of social worker and client or others in the application of existing or available competence are more pertinent than the existence or the availability of competence.

Social work ethics does not inhere in social work competence but does require it. Neither does social work ethics standardize competence. This seems analogous to Heinz Hartmann's (1960) assertion that

---

[2]For a discussion of accountability to employers, see chapter 14.

even among psychoanalysts who have not only undergone analysis but in their therapeutic activities follow more or less the same professional code, we find representatives of different "Weltanschauungen" and corresponding differences in their general moral codes [pp. 84–85].

The social worker's professional ethics must transcend his personal ethics when the two are not entirely reconcilable. For this purpose, he needs to be aware of his own values and behavioral preferences, including those that arise out of his social, economic, and religious identification (Hartmann, pp. 55–63).

Social work ethics is not "bound to a particular view of existence," to use Edel's (1962) phrase, or to a fixed philosophical or religious system, though it may have been influenced by them in many ways. Edel's frame of reference is broader than the one that guides this discussion, but he captures much of the spirit of the present framework in the following statement:

In philosophical ethics, as is generally known, most ethical theories for the greater part of western philosophy were bound to a particular view of existence. Ancient theories were teleological; they tried to read off men's morals from an account of the purposive nature of man. Religious philosophies also were teleological, with divinity prescribing the human purposes. Where scientific trends grew, they sought to outline how men's strivings and obligations followed from their constitution and the laws governing their constitution. Only from Kant's time onwards do we find explicit attempts at securing the complete independence of ethics. In Kant, its "autonomy" means dismissing empirical considerations. In typical twentieth-century forms . . . it is primarily an argument for the independence of ethical judgment from theological, metaphysical, and scientific, in brief any existential pictures of the world and its necessities. It is a revolt from bondage in ethical decision [p. 70].

Social work ethics is not free-floating, however; nor does it operate in vacuo since it derives its form and substance from the social work service situation. It provides a framework for the social worker's ethical decisions—that is, his choices of actions, gestures, words, silences, and so on —which relate specifically to the moral implications of his service function and responsibility and to the obligations they connote.

The ethical issues that arise in the social worker's practice usually cannot be resolved without contending with a multiplicity of diverse, sometimes conflicting interests. His choice of action represents in effect the higher valuation of one or another of these interests. A leaning or concession in the direction of one interest may mean an offense or deprivation in the direction of another. If his choices can not be measured, they are weighted. What he must especially be on guard against is allowing his own interests to intrude on his client's. Sometimes, however, the choice is not between himself and his client but between his client and somebody else. This scarcely reduces the tension he experiences. His capacity for keen judgment and ethical conduct is then put to an extraordinary test. Social work ethics is designed to help him meet that test.

Social work ethics is necessarily an idealization of professional conduct, even though expectations in concurrently affected arenas sometimes conflict with one another. A child's interests may not coincide with the interests of his parents, and yet the interests of both may merit the social worker's earnest ethical consideration. Or the interests of a client may not coincide with those of the social worker's employing agency, although the social worker incurs professional obligations to both. And so on. The idealized expectations, even when they apply to cases that are not at all moot, may be beyond the capacity of any social worker alive. But each social worker is obliged to stretch his ethical capacity to its boundary and go on developing it. That too is the social worker's ethical responsibility.

But what about social workers whose limited capacity perseveres? Provision must be made for them, either to help them grow in their capacity or to restrict the freedom of their ethical movement. If there are risks in this view, there are also risks to clients and others if some kind of controls or alternatives are lacking.

Therefore, regulation and education become pertinent considerations. Short of these, or to the extent that they prove insufficient, the problem of entry into the profession must be addressed. Kant (1963) once suggested that "the child ought not to exercise greater powers than are in keeping with its years [p. 249]." And Socrates demonstrated to Lysis (Edman, 1956, pp. 8–11) that only when a person has displayed the wisdom and capacity to manage the affairs of others can such affairs be safely entrusted to him. Cannot the same be said for social workers who are permitted entry into the sanctum of the social worker-client relationship? Must it not! Here too there are risks and dilemmas: Who will make these judgments? On what grounds? With what safeguards for the social worker? Etc. Etc. But can the matter be validly neglected?

For those who are already practicing, some guides to ethical conduct are indeed available, although they are not in all respects definitive, refined, or enforceable. They can be considered under several broad headings—the social worker, the client, third parties, the social worker's colleagues, the social worker's employer, and society—which are discussed in the following chapters.

Chapter 10

SOCIAL WORK ETHICS: THE SOCIAL WORKER[1]

What is it reasonable to expect of the social worker in light of his professional responsibility, his clients' need for help, the extent to which his clients subject themselves to hazards in the quest for help, and the community's or the government's sanctioning of the social worker's freedom to provide it? There are no laws or commandments that dictate or even sufficiently explicate the expectations which might be validly entertained by peers, clients, or governmental authorities, let alone be employed as a basis of control over the practice of social workers or as a basis for adjudicating grievances and charges against them.

There is a code of social work ethics, but it is far from definitive and it is still in the stage of emergence.[2] It is

[1]This chapter and those that follow draw freely from Levy (1974c).
[2]The National Association of Social Workers is in fact currently in the process of revising its code of ethics (*NASW News,* January, 1975, and May, 1975).

certainly not inclusive or conclusive, nor is it extensively monitored or enforced.

On the other hand, there is sufficient access to an understanding of the nature of social work—differences in preference or emphasis notwithstanding—and of professional responsibility, as well as the context of social work practice at all levels of professional responsibility, to permit the projection of social work ethics in its various dimensions.

The first dimension of social work ethics to consider is that of the social worker himself. How he comports himself in terms of his professional responsibility and how responsive he is to the trust and reliance placed in him by clients and others are matters of social work ethics. Aside from specific ethical responsibilities to specific clients and other persons and organizations to whom he may be said to owe professional and hence ethical responsibility, the social worker has ethical responsibilities that relate to his being and behavior in general, no matter whom these may affect. In other words, ethical principles can be formulated which apply to the being and behavior of the social worker himself as a member of his professional community and as a member of a profession that carries serious social responsibility to persons and institutions.

These principles are not necessarily conceded or adopted by the social work profession, though some are. They are simply proposed as prescriptive principles that make sense, considering what the social worker does in the line of professional duty, with whom he does it, for whom he does it, and the circumstances under which he does it.

Much of the insight that guides the formulation of these principles as well as those offered in the following chapters derives from an analysis of existing codes of ethics (Levy, 1972b) and the filtering of their provisions through the social work screen, with the purpose of determining which principles apply to the social work service situation and the social work profession and in what kind of formulation. Sometimes it is not only a question of which ethical principles seem applicable to social work but a question of how they are formulated. At any rate, these principles are not proposed with any finality, although they are offered with some conviction about their relevance to and utility for social work.

A major, if not a prerequisite expectation for the social worker, and one for which each social worker should feel special ethical responsibility, is competence. Competence refers not only to the social worker's initial professional equipment when he undertakes social work responsibility as a full-fledged practitioner but to something beyond that. As an ethical responsibility rather than simply as a description or judgment of the social worker's professional ability, aptitude, and capacity, competence is charged with a moral dimension in the sense that the social worker is expected to feel obliged to be specifically equipped to perform the specific function he undertakes as well as to undertake social work service in the first place.

To borrow the conclusion of a study committee of the American Psychological Association (1953) after an investigation of a large number of "critical incidents" in the variegated practices of psychologists: "It is unethical for . . . [a social worker] to offer service outside his area of training and experience or beyond the boundaries of his competence [p. 44]." This statement suggests that the practitioner must be adequately acquainted with the standards of the profession, competent to practice the profession, and adequately prepared for any change of function or responsibility within the broad range of the professional franchise or sanction. He must avoid any pretense of competence which he does not truly possess in a specific realm of practice despite his agency or institutional affiliation, his association with social workers or social work services, or the circumstantial appearances of a given situation.

The range of possible services within the social work profession is rather broad. This means that the social worker must assume the ethical responsibility for determining when he is and when he is not qualified to serve a client unless an employing agency, supervisor, or other instrument of social control determines that beforehand or monitors it afterwards.

A person who pretends to be a social worker when he is not is an imposter and therefore violates a general ethical principle as well as a principle of social work ethics for it is unethical for anyone to pretend to be what he is not, especially if he proceeds on that basis to act with and toward others as if he were that which he is not. A person who has gained sanctioned entry into the social work profession has sufficient freedom of motion in serving clients and otherwise affecting them and others to require considerable judgment concerning what he does in his professional capacity and must do to become equipped to do it. Alternatively, he must know when to refer a client to someone else, better or more suitably equipped to deal with him, and to act on that knowledge, not with abandon but with full recognition that it is his responsibility to do so, either because he cannot do what needs doing or because it is not his but someone else's function to do it. When any of these alternatives to intervention with a client are indicated and the social worker proceeds nevertheless to intervene, he is engaging in unethical conduct. He is not adhering to the ethical strictures of professional competence and responsibility. Moreover, the implied objective is the maintenance and enrichment of the social worker's competence. The worker is expected to be able not only to serve his clients competently but to serve them at the highest levels of competence of which he is *and can become* capable.

Whatever it is that a social worker may be called on in his professional capacity to know and to do, he is expected, according to the principle of competence, to assume responsibility for knowing and doing. He is expected to acquire such knowledge and skill as may be needed to provide the right service at the right time if he does not already possess them. He is expected to feel the professional obligation to keep up-to-date with the growing knowledge of his profession and the growing knowledge that is relevant to it and hence to assume the ethical responsibility for doing something about it.

Whatever the social worker's foundation of general social work knowledge and skill, he is expected—that is, it is his ethical responsibility—to become specifically prepared and equipped to help clients meet their specific needs as long as those needs are reasonably related to the social worker's professional function. Thus careful study of a case, exploration of a client's need or problem, or investigation of the available modes and prerequisites of intervention—including concepts and theories as well as resources and facilities applicable to the need or problem—is assumed to be the social worker's ethical responsibility. The social worker is ethically accountable not only for what he does and the way in which he does it but for what he might have been reasonably expected to *consider* doing but for his lack of awareness of what he might have done and his lack of initiative in discovering it.

The social worker should know what he is capable of and what he is not capable of and accordingly make the appropriate choice or provision—withdrawal, referral, counsel, guidance, consultation, and so forth—in the best interests of clients and anybody else toward whom he has attributable responsibility.

Doing only what one is competent to do is in many respects equatable with doing what one is authorized and empowered to do and what it is one's function to do. But one may have the competence to do something and still be ethically obliged *not* to do it. A social worker, as a matter of ethics, is expected to stick to his professional last, even if he can cope with other lasts. He is ethically obliged to do only that which he is appointed to do and what clients and the public are entitled to expect him to do on the basis of societally defined or understood occupational functions. This does not mean that the social worker inflexibly ignores emergencies. A prime hallmark of the professional practitioner is the responsible and timely exercise of judgment, particularly in emergencies in which clients' needs, and perhaps their lives and health, must be regarded as paramount. A departure from this principle must be clearly acknowledged as such, however, and last no longer than is absolutely essential to safeguard a client's well-being.

2. Integrity is another expectation for which the social worker must assume particular responsibility. The essence of this principle is that as a member of the social work profession, the social worker owes it to himself and his profession as well as his clients to deal with clients and the public alike in a manner that will validate the trust and confidence placed in him and his profession. According to this principle of integrity, the social worker must do nothing in his professional capacity that will raise any question about the trustworthiness and competence of himself or his peers or cause any doubt about the confidence and reliance placed in him and his peers.

It is the better part of the social worker's integrity for him not to say or do anything publicly without having an adequate basis in fact, understanding, or conviction for doing so. He must even avoid assuming a position or a responsibility that could conceivably cast a shadow on his integrity. It should be ever and always apparent to all that the social worker is guided by a zeal to serve his client and the public responsibly and well and by the awareness that his position as a social worker requires certain constraints and limits which are not normally required of ordinary citizens in private capacities. This implies the expectation of exemplary and carefully considered behavior, an eye always on the look-out for how the behavior may be perceived by others and how it may reflect on the social worker or his profession.

There can be little doubt that the principle of integrity, like other ethical principles, implies some loss of freedom on the social worker's part. The worker becomes accountable for what he does and does not do and what he has the opportunity to do or not do, not only in his relationship with clients, but in his status and capacity as a social worker in other connections. Because he is a social worker, he is no longer free to do what he chooses without considering its impact on his performance or standing as a social worker. His professional life is, as it were, open to inspection.

An issue that will be contended with in greater detail below is the relevance of the social worker's behavior to his professional performance and capacity. What about his right to privacy and to the freedom to be and do whatever he chooses to be and do in his private capacity? He can hardly be said to lose all his rights as a person, citizen, and private human being just because he has chosen to become a social worker. Some of these rights he does sacrifice, but must he sacrifice all his rights? It would seem that the ethical principle of integrity does not connote an invasion of the social worker's realm as a private citizen, although sometimes the line between the professional and private realm cannot be sharply drawn.

For the moment, perhaps, the criterion of relevance may be asserted as a caution against enslaving the social worker in an all-embracing bondage of social work responsibility. That is more than can be reasonably expected of any social worker, and his rewards hardly justify such an extreme sacrifice. At the same time, the nature of social work responsibility and the ethics it requires do occasion some sacrifice of autonomy.

Socrates' (Edman, 1956) expression of the principle of relevance has not been improved:

> What sort of doing is good in letters? and what sort of doing makes a man good in letters? Clearly the knowing of them. And what sort of well-doing makes a man a good physician? Clearly the knowledge of the art of healing the sick. "But he who does ill is the bad." Now, who becomes a bad physician? Clearly he who is in the first place a physician, and in the second place a good physician; for he may become a bad one also; but none of us unskilled individuals can by any amount of doing ill become physicians, any more than we can become carpenters or anything of that sort; and he who by doing ill cannot become a physician at all, clearly cannot become a bad physician [p. 238].

The social worker's integrity is not appraised on the basis of standards of general conduct but on the basis of standards that are relevant to his practice and standing as a social worker.

④ Closely related to the principle of integrity is the expectation or necessity of dignity. The gist of this principle is that the social worker comports himself in a manner that upholds the dignity and honor of the social work profession and brings credit to it. It is beneath the dignity of the social worker and his profession to recruit clients or compete for an assignment. Role implications figure importantly in this matter of professional dignity. The social worker must avoid acting the clown in his professional capacity or in his role as a member of the social work profession. Even the reckless use of profanity is subject to censure, as is any indiscretion that might conceivably discredit the profession or the worker himself as a representative of it.

⑤ Impartiality is another important requisite as far as the social worker as a social worker is concerned. This principle is addressed to the social worker's behavior and attitude toward clients as a group rather than to particular clients whom he has undertaken to help or serve. The social worker is expected to serve any client who may require his service, and in the manner in which the client requires it, with neither fear nor favor; without regard to race, creed, color, or national origin; and without a biased regard for circumstances that affect the client and might affect the prospects for a successful outcome in relation to the client's need or request for service. An apt illustration of this is the social worker's obligation toward a psychotic, terminally ill, or resistant client. The principle of impartiality implies that the social worker is ready to take on any and all comers who may need his service and talents no matter how pessimistic the prognosis or arduous the attempt.

The social worker must reckon with his attitudes toward certain kinds of clients or certain approaches to working with them. Aside from some of the more obvious racial, religious, or personal prejudices and biases that cause a social worker to prejudge or deprive clients, there are attitudes of a more subtle nature that make the social worker insufficiently responsive to his ethical responsibility for impartiality. Attitudes of a subversive nature in this connection may stem, for example, from something so wholesome (relatively speaking) as a conviction about a particular practice modality or from something so intense as a moral judgment or sheer personal disgust about a client's traits or characteristics. The effect may well be a vindictive, constricting, punitive, or other equally intrusive response to a client, which at least deprives him of due service and may have devastating consequences.

In a word, it is unethical for a social worker to permit any attitude or reaction he may have toward a client, the client's need, or an available service approach to intrude on his competence, readiness or capacity to serve the client. It is unethical for the practitioner to be influenced by any personal reaction that is not conducive or is antithetical to adequately performing his service function and to making available to the client anything that would best serve the client's interests and needs (e.g., Kahn, 1961; Kantor, 1966). Nor can there be much doubt that despite unctuous characterizations to the contrary (e.g., the often-heard remark that "charity patients get better care than the most affluent private patient"), "free clinic," ward patients, welfare clients, and others served by social workers suffer a number of relative deprivations. Yerby's (1966) commentary on health care has its analogues in social work practice.

> Health care of the disadvantaged is many things.[3] It is frequently inadequate, sometimes quite poor, provided with little dignity or compassion, and rarely related to the total needs of the individual or family. These things are certainly not true of health care in general in the United States. . . . The pervasive stigma of charity permeates our arrangements for health care for the disadvantaged and whether the program is based upon the private practice of medicine or upon public or nonprofit clinics and hospitals, it tends to be piecemeal, poorly supervised, and uncoordinated. Those who provide the service tend to focus their attention on the episode of disease or even the symptom, defending their actions on the grounds that they are poorly paid by the public welfare agency, or that their mission of teaching and research must come first [pp. 6–7].[4]

The principle of impartiality is not premised on the issue of whether the social worker stands to gain—if only in sheer gratification of his impulses or coddling of his biases—from a deviation from it. A departure from the principle is weighed simply on the basis of any influence on the social worker that prevents him from addressing his full

[3]"The term 'disadvantaged' is a contemporary euphemism for the poor. We employ euphemisms to shield ourselves from the harshness of reality [p. 5]."
[4]In a survey conducted by the New York City Bar Association, it was found that "the lower the status of the clientele, the higher the rate of violation [of ethical norms] by members of the bar [Carlin, 1966, p. 66]."

and unbiased attention to the needs of and service to any class of clientele. This includes the influence of the client's failure to pay for the social worker's service, of the involuntary nature of the service, or of the client's status as a nonpaying recipient of service.

Many influences may taint the social worker's impartiality and deprive clients of their due as a consequence. If subject to these influences, whether internal or external, the social worker is not likely to be as impartial as his ethics as a social worker requires. The effect is the loss of what has been described as the practitioner's independence.[5]

> Independence, in the sense of being self-reliant, not subordinate, is essential to the practice of all professions. No self-respecting professional man ... will subordinate his professional judgment to the views of his patient or client. He cannot evade his professional responsibility for the advice, opinions and recommendations which he offers. If his patients or clients do not like what he says, the practitioner may regret it, but no one will condone his changing his honest opinion in order to avoid giving offense or to secure his fee. ... Independence in this sense means avoidance of situations which would tend to impair objectivity or permit personal bias to influence delicate judgments. ... It is primarily a condition of mind and character. ... It has been recognized that the appearance of lack of independence may be almost as damaging as the reality [Carey & Doherty, 1966, pp. 38–39; see also, Croxton-Smith 1965, b, pp. 242–243].

Many influences conspire to compromise the social worker's impartiality and could result in the social worker's failure to make the full measure of his professional skill and

[5]This concept should not be confused with the concept of independence or autonomy as it is sometimes discussed in the social work literature, where it represents a reaction "to the old problem of oversupervision in social work [Epstein, 1973; compare Haug & Sussman, 1969)."

judgment available to clients.[6] The critical ethical concern is the worker's readiness to devote himself completely to "the welfare of the individual and group served ["Profession of social work"]."

The client, as Dembo (1970) suggested, remains an important source of the social worker's understanding of the client's problem or need, and he must be credited in the selection of the social worker's interventions. Extraneous influences that induce the social worker to neglect the client's authoritativeness as a relevant impetus to professional judgment must be resisted. On the other hand, the social worker must also be impartial enough to resist the client's own emotional intimidations and demands when the failure to do so may reduce the client's access to the social worker's maximum professional capacity, judgment, and resources. Excessive identification with a client as well as insufficient identification subjects the social worker to the risk of losing his impartiality. Guilt about a client's deprivations (a white social worker's guilt concerning black clients, for example) as well as a pernicious though undetected racism can easily disarm the social worker of his otherwise available armamentarium of practice principles, more judiciously calculated to help the client solve his problems or meet his needs. A moralistic inclination can similarly derail a social worker who serves drug addicts or sexually promiscuous adolescents.

[6]To avoid possible ambiguity, it must be emphasized that the focus here is on the social worker and the extent to which he does or does not make himself and his professional competence available to clients in general, either because of some characteristics which they share or because of the worker's responses to them, or because of the social worker's preoccupation with other loyalties, considerations, concerns, and so on. Once the social worker undertakes to serve a client, however, a degree of partiality is not amiss since he is presumably concerned about and represents those interests and needs of the client that are legitimately related to his professional responsibility.

Whether the social worker does too little for a client who reaps his disapproval or too much for a client who arouses his indiscriminate protective instincts, the ethical problem to which the social worker must be alert is insufficient impartiality to address himself to the needs of his clients, whoever they are. The worker is obligated to make available to his clients whatever, in his best and freest judgment, he regards as "right" for them on grounds of agency and professional function, service, and long- as well as short-range practice goals.

Privileged clients are as hazardous a stimulus in this connection as disadvantaged ones. The "special" client, one whose characteristics or situation disproportionately generates the social worker's subjectivity, and the V.I.P., the client whose occupational position or social status prevents the worker from regarding him as the client in need he truly may be, can cause the social worker to lose enough of his perspective to render him incapable of retaining mastery over his own professional soul. The result may be that he does not concentrate his professional thought and effort on either the client's interests or the service he is professionally obliged to provide (cf. Pollack & Battle, 1963, and Weintraub, 1964).

The social worker's employing agency can also be a disruptive factor as far as the social worker's impartiality is concerned.[7] The agency's communal, financial, ideological, and other commitments can easily distort the social worker's practice focus. The worker is subject, and must avoid becoming a party to unwritten agency preferences and biases that militate against the fulfillment of his professional obligations toward clients. The predominating val-

---

[7]The private practitioner is not entirely exempt from this influence. Although not manifestly accountable to an agency, he is nevertheless subject to the subversive effects of landlord, neighbors, office structure, co-tenants, and the like.

ues of the surrounding community have a similar effect if the social worker responds to them or identifies with them to the point of neglecting his clients' legitimate interests and differences.

The social worker himself may serve as his own adversary in this regard. Any personal inclinations that contribute to the loss of his impartiality require his studious quest "for the conscious control of his unconscious [Grotjohn, 1972, p. 468]" if he is to avoid inadvertently pitting his own interests against those of his clients. The social worker may not be aware of his responses to his clients. If so, he can hardly be confident about his capacity to control them sufficiently to function freely and maximally in his clients' behalf. And his ethics may become a matter of considerable uncertainty as a result (e.g., Bugental, 1964; Fromm-Reichmann, 1950; Savage, 1961).

Whether the social worker's exploitation of clients in relation to axes of his own he wishes to grind is done consciously or unconsciously, his impartiality is tarnished. He may find himself acting out with his clients his grievances against his agency, superiors, and colleagues and sandwiching his clients in between opposing forces as a result (Schneider, 1963). At the very least, his clients may end up at the short end of the service stick.

The social worker's drive for his own success and productivity, whether institutionally induced or self-motivated, can be another subversive influence insofar as his impartiality is concerned. Clients thus become victims rather than objects of the social worker's ministrations because the social worker responds to them as though it is more important for him that clients change or improve than it is for them. Dembo (1970) provides a penetrating analogue in this connection—"Whose problem should be alleviated, the investigator's or the sufferer's? Who really knows how it hurts, when it hurts more, or when it starts to hurt less [p. 2]?"

The social worker's imposition of his values on clients is another manifestation of the loss of impartiality. This is an ethical departure with a practical consequence for if the social worker is extremely busy with his own values and attitudes, he is less available to give his attention to his clients' values and attitudes and how they may affect the need, problem, or service to which the social worker should be addressing himself. Therefore, the principle of impartiality has many ramifications and is in many respects a rather nuclear ethical principle.

But a final principle affecting the practitioner, deserves mention before we end this chapter, because it too carries many implications. More seriously, perhaps, it generates many conflicts and issues that will be considered later. This principle is that of propriety. What it requires of the social worker is scrupulous representation of high standards of personal (often read as moral) conduct. The general ethical judgment to be avoided as a consequence of the social worker's behavior in his private life is whether the questionable conduct he is capable of outside the social work service situation he may be capable of *in* it. Nothing that the social worker does, this principle implies, should be capable of generating public doubt about his honesty or morality as a practitioner. Here too, however, the boundary between the social worker's personal liberty and professional responsibility must be carefully and discriminately drawn.

This issue affects as well the related expectation that the social worker will retain possession of his faculties, certainly while he is on professional duty and perhaps even when he is not. The essence of this principle, aside from any implications of temperance (and the issue of relevance to professional role and status must also be contended with in this connection), is that at no time when a social worker is performing his professional function, representing it, or subject to a call to do so, should he fail to be in full command of his mental and physical capacities. Under such circumstances, he is enjoined against drunkenness, drug addiction, or other impediments to self-control.

Short of the necessary delineation between the social worker's personal and professional self, this chapter has summarized what the social worker, as a matter of ethical responsibility, is expected to be and represent in his practice as a social worker and in his representation of the social work profession. This expectation may sound like a fanciful idealization of the unlikely: no human being could be so angelic and still have the flesh and spirit—the humanity, if you will—that are often demanded of real-life social workers. Yet it is not an entirely unrealistic reflection of the seriousness of social work responsibility and of the urgency of the social worker's ethical being as well as behaving.

Chapter 11

SOCIAL WORK ETHICS: THE CLIENT

Social work ethics is primarily addressed to concern for the client. Although other categories of ethics affect the social worker's relationship to other persons and institutions, directly or ultimately they have some import for the social worker's actual or prospective clients. When the quality of service rendered to them is not at stake, their rights, autonomy, dignity, opportunities, or something else of value or consequence to them is.

Some of the ethical principles that are proposed in relation to clients are similar and even identical to those that have been proposed in relation to the social worker himself. Their operation is different, however; what is of concern here is the effect of the social worker's ethics on specific clients rather than the implications of the social worker's conduct and comportment for clients or prospective clients in general.

The social worker is ethically accountable, not only for what he does in his professional relationship with his client, but for what he does not do that the relationship gives him the opportunity and responsibility to do. He is also accountable for the way in which he does or does not do it. Accountability implies some loss of freedom on the social worker's part, because he is not only not free to do what he wishes when he undertakes service to a client; he is also not free *not* to do what he can do, on the one hand, in fulfilling his professional mission with the client and, on the other, in responding to the client's rights and prerogatives.

These rights and prerogatives are obviously not all-inclusive, but they must be carefully considered to the extent that any invasion of them may be an inadvertent or unjustifiable consequence of the social worker's service. The social worker-client relationship is in many ways a strategic encounter with stakes of greater or lesser consequence to the client very much within the purview of the social worker's control and very much a function of the client's need for service or subjection to it. The hazards to the client must, in the last analysis, be avoided primarily by the social worker. It is the worker who must be alert to the ethical problems posed by the social work service situation, and it is chiefly he who must seek the key to their solution. The worker is thus accountable for ethical as well as competent practice.

This implies, first, an extraordinarily high standard of care and, second, considerable initiative (cf. Levy, 1968). As a matter of ethical as well as competent practice, the social worker volunteers his efforts; he does not wait until they are demanded. This does not mean that he inflicts himself on his clients. The better part of his respect for them is to insure for them a measure of autonomy. But whatever his clients have a right to get, it is up to him to see that they have ready access to it without waiting to discover whether they know they have a right to it. If a welfare client, for example, is unaware of his right to a clothing allotment and therefore does not claim it, it is the social worker's ethical responsibility to tell him about the allotment and facilitate his acquiring it, whatever the inconvenience for the worker or his employing agency.

Lewis (1972) has underscored the connection between the social worker's exercise of this kind of initiative and the trust of clients, which we have said forms an essential link in the chain of consequences of social work ethics:

> Failure to reach eligible populations in need with information of their rights and opportunities reinforces in them a deep disbelief in the intentions of those offering a service and distrust of procedures used to determine eligibility for the service [p. 410].

The social worker's ethics in relation to the client is not designed to generate or preserve the client's trust, however. It is instead a response to professional obligations, owed to the client in his own right and hence intrinsic to the social worker-client relationship. Although the social worker's ethics requires that he consider the effects of his conduct on the trust and confidence of clients in general, his ethics in relation to his clients is a response to specific duties owed them in particular. It is a reflection of his concern about the way his conduct—or nonconduct— affects his clients and about the way in which he deals with and treats them.

One ethical principle that guides the social worker has been identified in the codes of ethics of a number of human service professions as devotion and loyalty to the client. This principle is often regarded as a "primary" duty, and it emphasizes the extent of the social worker's obligations to his client in that the social worker is expected to provide his client with the best qualitative and quantitative care, protection, and service of which he is capable. And while providing them, he is expected to treat the client with empathy, consideration, and fidelity. Devotion and loyalty require the social worker to apply himself to the maximum extent of his capacity, not only to safeguard the client's interests, but to advance the client's cause as far as his knowledge, skill, and ethics permit. This obviously makes possible some conflicts of loyalty when the social worker feels concurrent and unequivocal professional obligations to others—an issue that must be given some attention later on.

Still, considering the fact that the client comes, or is sent to the social worker for help or service and that he incurs hazards in the process—the hazard of not getting the help or service he needs or is led to expect and the hazard of getting it in a way that penalizes him—a degree of priority in his behalf is not unreasonable, although the social worker may be moved by other imperatives not to accord such priority under particular circumstances.

Whether the social worker carries professional assignments with individuals or groups; committees, boards or staffs; or community organizations or institutions, he has both the opportunity and responsibility to represent and, often, to plead the cause of his clientele. In his working relationships with them, it may be incumbent on him to sustain his "affective neutrality," which is kin to the principle of "objectivity" that will be discussed shortly.

> The person who brings his problems to a social worker . . . is in trouble. His emotions will be aroused by this, and intensified by internal resentment at having to expose his weakness to an outsider. This situation confronts the professional "helper" with something of a dilemma. If he becomes emotionally involved himself he loses objectivity, his ability to see facts in clear perspective, and his power to help; but at the same time a sufficiently close relationship must be established to convince the client of the worker's identification with his problem and of willingness to understand and help. There must be involvement and no involvement at the same time [Wilensky & Lebeaux, 1958, p. 300].

The major reason for the social worker's affective neutrality is to avoid depriving the client of the completely free and deliberate attention that the worker owes him. The worker must also be sure not to deprive the client of the will and responsibility to solve problems associated with his own behavior and aspirations. In helping the client cope with external conditions and institutions that affect his circumstances and opportunities, however, the social worker is shamelessly biased, at times to the point of engaging with the client in open alliance and alignments.

In his working relationship with his client, the social worker provides data, suggests alternatives, and contemplates consequences so that the client has an adequate basis for sound decision-making which is maximally congruent with his preferences and interests. In representing his client's interests in relation to impinging environmental forces, the social worker commits himself to outcomes that advance those interests.

Within the framework of agency function and professional responsibility, the social worker, in devotion and loyalty to his client, defends and represents the client within agencies, including his own, and outside them to the extent that agencies and others do not give the client his due. He also defends and represents his client when agencies and others are guided by policies and practices that are not in the client's best interests (Levy, 1974a).

The social worker should see a client through to the end—unless the client himself chooses to terminate the relationship when he is free to do so—or at least make adequate provision to ensure that the client continues to receive the care and attention he may need. The social worker must perform his tasks thoroughly. He must do so even when his investment of time, energy, and talent are disproportionate to his rewards.

Devotion and loyalty to his client preclude the serving

of two masters with conflicting interests. Therefore, the social worker must avoid ties or relationships that militate against his giving the client the full measure of his attention. This applies as well to other extracurricular responsibilities that might conceivably intrude on his client's prerogatives and the priority that is the client's due.

(2)   As already intimated, another important ethical principle involves objectivity toward clients. The social worker is enjoined, according to this principle, against letting extraneous interests or biases affect his professional decisions and actions in relation to his client. This principle is one of the bases for the injunction against service to friends and relatives. Emotional identification with a client, as already suggested, is a threat to objectivity. Any risk of insufficient objectivity may mean less than the best service or less than the unbiased service that the social worker can offer a client and that the client may need from him.

Excessive identification with a practice philosophy or school of thought may prove a possible deprivation to a client if the social worker's commitment to it results in a failure to avail the client of the benefits of another mode or regimen of service. A philosophic preference, in other words, may be a social worker's privilege, but only insofar as it does not result in arbitrarily or unreasonably ruling out something that may be in a client's best interest.

The social worker must be on guard against feelings about a client that might cause the client to be short-changed. The client's beliefs, inclinations, circumstances, or feelings, no matter how contradictory or alien they are to the social worker, must be respected. Although the worker need not invariably endorse them, he must ensure the attention that the client requires—and in an unprejudiced, unbegrudging, and wholehearted manner. Negative attitudes toward his client or toward the client's behavior and way of life are likely to bar the social worker's objectivity. Vindictive, constrictive, moralistic, or punitive reactions to a client are, in this context, unethical. Such reactions may be less a function of the client's behavior patterns or life-style than the social worker's conviction that the client needs to experience the "good life," and they may be equally offensive from an ethical point of view. From this point of view, a social worker's umbrage at a welfare recipient who refuses to submit to "counseling" as a precondition for receiving public assistance is as intrusive as a worker's judgmental attitude toward the unwed mother who bears an additional child while dependent on the public treasury.

The social worker must also take care lest he is moved to act more by greed or the quest for personal gratification than by the unhampered conviction that a client needs his help and requires full access to it as well as the social worker's objective professional judgment (cf., Lowe, 1959).

The social worker must be especially sensitive to how his own psyche may impede his objectivity. It is the rare social worker who can be aware of all his psychodynamic responses to his clients and what his clients may feel, do, or say, let alone master them (Hartmann, 1960, pp. 84–92). Nevertheless, he is ethically accountable for restraining his personal needs and anxieties that could otherwise divest him of his objectivity. To paraphrase Grossman's (1964, p. 67) characterization of what he regards as "crucial" for the therapist, the social worker must have enough presence of mind and control over his anxieties to permit rational decisions when dealing with the client's reactions, always keeping in mind the client's welfare rather than his own.

The principle of objectivity does not rely on the supposition that the social worker, any more than any other mortal, can overcome his own self-interest, whatever other provocations to the loss of objectivity he may be subject to. Nevertheless, he must try to do so if he is to be capable of ethical practice in these terms. And it is possible, if we are to believe Dostoevsky (1956) when he says:

> Man everywhere and at all times, whoever he may be, has
> preferred to act as he chose and not in the least as his reason
> and advantage dictated. And one may choose what is con-
> trary to one's own interests, and sometimes one *positively*
> *ought* (that is my idea) [p. 71].

The social worker, for one, "positively ought," as is implicit
in the social work practice principle of consciously using
oneself as a social worker—a principle for which social
workers have been held professionally accountable (cf.,
Hamilton, 1954; Grossbard, 1954).

(3) Honesty and candor is another ethical principle to
which the social worker is bound in relation to his clients.
The worker owes his client the truth, even if it hurts, but
not *in order* to hurt his client. Some circumstances do not
require candor so much as a kindly statement of the facts,
with provision for possible consequences of the statement
for the client. The social worker must often call a client's
attention to the adverse effects of a possible course of action or the prospect of adverse effects in the absence of
action. It is his obligation under this principle neither to
exaggerate nor minimize a client's condition or prospects.
The objective is not to sadistically pummel the client with
hard facts, but to help the client realistically appraise his
situation and the consequences of available alternatives.

The social worker should not lead the client to believe
that he has more to offer than he in fact does, and he should
acknowledge to the client the limits of what he can do as
well as what the client may have to do for himself. If the
worker is accountable to persons or institutions other than
the client, he ought to reveal as much. The client should
not be misled into thinking that he or his confidences are
safe with the social worker if in any respect they are not. A
deception out of kindness to a client is no more ethical than
a deception out of reckless disregard, although some circumstances require a touch of discretion concerning
whether, when, and how a truth will be disclosed. But the

ethical principle of honesty and candor stands, although the question of the art of revelation may remain to tax the social worker's professional skill. With respect to circumstances such as a client's terminal illness or self-destructive behavior patterns, the issue is not how promptly the social worker should impetuously blurt out the truth without preparation but how much information should be shared, in what manner, when, toward what service end, and relevant to which of the client's needs.

Halleck (1963) has described as dishonest and deceptive and, consequently, as an intrusion on the practitioner's responsibility to his client a series of "lies" inflicted on disturbed adolescents that would tend to violate the principle of honesty and candor. Practitioners "entrusted with the professional management of disturbed adolescents," he says, may often be communicating "information, values and morals to adolescent clients that they do not believe fully [p. 48]." He suggests that they may be precipitating rebellious behavior as a result of their "failure to present themselves and their world in an honest, straightforward manner [p. 48]."

Halleck refers specifically to the lie of adult morality ("[Practitioners] . . . imply that adults control their impulses and that success in the world is dependent upon such restraint [p. 49]," which, if it is true at all, is true to but a limited extent); the lie of professional helpfulness ("the worker pretends that his only motivation" is to help the client, when he may actually be an agent of the community, which "wants him to control, attenuate, or in some way modify the behavior of an individual who is causing it some distress [p. 49]"); the lie of confidentiality ("the worker behaves as though the adolescent is entitled to expect confidentiality and as though it were going to be provided [p. 50]," when the worker is in no position to guarantee it); the lie of rewards for conformity ("if the adolescent is told that the simple expedient of conforming to adult standards produces pleasure, he is told a lie [p. 51]"); the lie of denying limitations ("many workers fail to see that with a few exceptions they are dealing with people of limited potential who will never be like them [p. 52]," or at least speak and act as they do); the lie of optimism ("professional workers are guilty . . . of continuously exhorting the adolescent to 'open up; trust me; if you rely on me and share things with me, all will go well [p. 52]"); and, finally, the lie of rationalizing dislike ("sometimes the worker's anger is totally denied but comes out only through his behavior toward the adolescent. . . . It is dishonest and unfair both to the worker and to the adolescent to deny, rationalize, or displace this anger [p. 53]").

The ethical connotations of this series of "lies" are quite evident, as is the fact that they violate the principle of honesty and candor. Nor are they less applicable, with but slight modification, to the social worker's relationship with clients who are neither disturbed nor adolescent.

The social worker is obviously not supposed to profit from what he acquires by way of information or revelations incidental to his relationship with the client, but the principle of honesty and candor does not rest on the benefit that the social worker derives from a deviation. Whatever merit he finds in the deviation, he is obliged to weigh scrupulously what he suggests or states to his client to insure that it does not misrepresent to or mislead the client about any fact or circumstance. And the suggestions or statements he does make should be made only after he has carefully considered them and validated them by careful study, thought, and exploration. As much as possible, they should be carefully calculated not to cloud or distort the mutual expectations between himself and his client.

But the principle of honesty and candor requires modulation. Nothing makes this so evident as the concept of confrontation, a mode of intervention in psychotherapy to which social workers seem to have a particular affinity.

It is, in effect, honesty and candor with a vengeance. There is no question but that confrontation does have its constructive uses as a form of professional intervention designed to make quite apparent to the client what is on the social worker's mind. It is often the treatment of choice, and it does have the appealing quality of spontaneity (e.g., Garner, 1960; Garner & Jeans, 1962). Words need not be used to resort to it, and it is ostensibly resorted to in relation to a client's need as the social worker perceives it at a given moment.

The trouble is that as a kind of catalyzed candor, confrontation is as capable of harm as it is of good. It makes discriminating use especially necessary because it can have shattering consequences for the client. No truer words are spoken than are sometimes uttered by a sadist, an authoritarian person, or a controlling individual whose confrontation may be motivated—perhaps unconsciously—less to accelerate a client's needed change than to disturb his equilibrium. The social worker who is promiscuously inclined to venture into a confrontation may simply enjoy seeing a client sweat, squirm, or dissolve in the face of an unwelcome or premature truth. Such a social worker may ingenuously perceive a ripe opening for a confrontation, but the *perception* may be more selective than his *use* of the technique and his passion for honesty and candor (cf., Reader, 1964).

(4) The principle of confidentiality, which has already been anticipated, is particularly important for the worker-client relationship. The social worker is obliged to maintain inviolate any confidence or information affecting his client that can, by the most minimal of criteria, be regarded as secret, personal, or private. The confidence or information may not be relevant to the social worker's service to the client, and it may not be revealed intentionally. However it comes to the social worker's attention, as long as it emerges in the course of and as a consequence of the social worker's

service to the client, it is not supposed to be shared with anyone else, unless the law absolutely and explicitly demands it or it can be unequivocally demonstrated that the client's well-being or the fundamental welfare of others is clearly and immediately at stake. When there is some such clear and evident justification for sharing confidential information, the social worker is bound to divulge only the data necessary to safeguard manifestly threatened life or well-being and only to the extent that responsibility for their protection may be reasonably attributed to the social worker.

When the communications between practitioner and client are privileged, the privilege is the client's, and only he can waive the right to keep the communications confidential. Otherwise, the social worker is bound by the principle of confidentiality (cf. Group for the Advancement of Psychiatry, 1960; National Conference of Lawyers and Social Workers, 1968; Richardson, 1955). The exceptions do make for some ambiguity (Hollender, 1956, p. 2). When there is any doubt and when the social worker is free to exercise his own judgment, he is obliged to adhere strictly to the principle of confidentiality.

In one sense, this principle may be summarized as the social worker's obligation to use the client's confidences for him, not against him, and to permit himself to receive confidences from the client only when he may be able to do something constructive with them—something consonant with his professional function and his professional responsibility to the client. In general, the social worker should either avoid confidences completely, when he fears they are not safe from exposure, or keep them secret in the absence of some obviously compelling reason not to—and then primarily in the service of the client himself.

5   The principle of propriety, which was discussed in the previous chapter, also governs behaviors that directly affect the social worker's clients. The behaviors involved are simi-

lar to those described in relation to the social worker as a member of the social work profession. However, the present context is the relationship between the social worker and his clients and the transactions between them. This principle applies to the social worker's condition and comportment *while practicing.* Sir Thomas Lund (1960) has made a useful distinction between professional misconduct (which applies here) and unprofessional conduct. The former he describes as specifically connected with professional functioning; the latter, as simply "unapproved" personal conduct. Thus a social worker who interviews a client while in a drunken stupor or while "high" on heroin, exceeds the boundaries of propriety in relation to service to his client. Furthermore, he deprives the client of competent professional attention. If he engages in sexual intercourse with his client he is also committing an impropriety since this too impairs the professional relationship that is a prerequisite to adequate and impartial service (compare Shor & Sanville, 1974). Less spectacular conduct can also offend the strictures of propriety: for example, overcharging the client, cheating him, or regaling him with obscenities.

(b)   The social worker owes his clients the duty of punctuality and expeditiousness. He is obliged to render his service to the client in the most appropriate and efficient manner possible (expeditiousness) and as promptly as possible (punctuality). If records must be maintained to guide those who need them to help the client, the social worker must see to it that such records are kept thoroughly and accurately. He must handle any necessary correspondence expeditiously. If the client's papers or assets are to be returned to him by the social worker or forwarded by the social worker to an authorized third party, the social worker should take care to perform these tasks promptly and thoroughly. If the client requires service or the administration of a procedure that the social worker is charged with, the social worker should effect it immediately and proficiently. If an expert, specialist, or superordinate person has been consulted on the client's behalf, the social worker should do everything in his power to facilitate the consultant's best performance. The principle of expeditiousness and punctuality enjoins the social worker against random experimentation with a client. If the social worker must experiment, it clearly must be the only available alternative, and the client, or someone authorized to act in his behalf if he lacks manifest capacity, must be consulted. The client's consent must be not merely informed but free: in other words, not the result of express or implied duress.

(n)   The objective of the principle of respect for the client's autonomy is to allow the client to make his own choices to the maximum extent that the situation and his competence permit. The social worker, in fact, must do all he can to make the situation as permissive as possible and to help the client to equip himself as well as he can to exercise his own judgment and initiative whenever and wherever practicable. This principle makes it incumbent on the social worker to "enable" the client to make his own decisions and to act for himself within the framework of existing law and policy —although the worker may also help him attempt to change them—and any other reasonable boundary within which the client, like any other free and responsible citizen, is obliged to stay. Enabling implies that the practitioner should provide or illuminate the facts the client will need to make intelligent and realistic decisions. He should clarify the available alternatives as well as the anticipated consequences—to the extent that the client needs his help to do so (Biestek, 1951; Bernstein, 1960; Keith-Lucas, 1963; Soyer, 1963).

(g)   The principle of personal attention is the counterpart of the principle of devotion and loyalty because it not only requires the social worker's devotion and loyalty to the client but requires it of him personally. Unsolicited delegation of professional responsibility is unethical, except for the obvious necessity of assigning tasks to employees and subordinates. These assignments must be limited, however, to tasks that are indeed amenable to confident delegation and must be entrusted only to qualified and carefully supervised personnel. The personal attention of the social worker assigned to or engaged by the client is the expectation, in the absence of some valid reason for delegation. The reassignment of clients to students and paraprofessional workers may be based on educational or other necessities, but it hardly tempers the principle. The social worker is not supposed to undertake responsibility with a client unless he expects to attend to it personally and stay with it. Neither should an agency make the assignment to him unless he means to do so. To take on more professional responsibility than one can handle well is censurable enough, ethically speaking, but to rely on apprentices, students, and other insufficiently prepared or equipped persons, and certainly to profit from their lower compensation, is an extreme offense.

This hardly exhausts the ethics of the social worker in relation to his clients, but it does reflect the reaches and purposes of social work ethics as far as clients are concerned. The social worker has extensive ethical responsibility toward his clients—*for* the provision of service, *in* the provision of the service, and in the conduct attending or affecting the service.

Chapter 12

SOCIAL WORK ETHICS: THIRD
PARTIES

Thus far the ethical responsibility of social workers toward clients and prospective clients has been emphasized. Even the emphasis on the worker's own conduct, irrespective of its impact on his clients, has been intended to suggest the concern the social worker ought to feel about the effect his behavior has, or may conceivably have on his capacity to be of service to clients and on the capacity of his profession to be of service to the community. The social worker has been importuned, through the prescription of sundry ethical principles, in effect, to be governed in his ethics by how his acts and omissions affect clients and the capacity of his profession to serve them. Although the prescribed ethical principles governing his behavior in his own right and in his relationship with clients have not been offered as a means of improving his professional practice, they have been guided by the judgment that the social worker's ethics need not conflict with the precepts of proficient social work practice. To the extent that social work practice is based on social work values, social work ethics should in fact be conducive to proficient practice. Nevertheless, social work ethics has not been rationalized as a means for ensuring effective practice; it has been regarded as transcendent and intransitive professional responsibility.

Similarly, effective social work practice has not been viewed as a guarantor of social work ethics. On the contrary, there are times when the social worker sacrifices practice efficiency for ethics. The client's rights and entitlements, from an ethical point of view, are often given precedence over his immediate service needs. There are indeed times and circumstances in the social worker's practice when what might work best in fulfilling his service goals on the client's behalf is accorded less priority than what he evaluates as more ethical in the light of other value-based obligations he owes to the client.

Still, very often the social worker's ethics serves as a factor in sound and proficient social work service. At least, there are many ways in which ethics reinforces good practice and good practice reinforces ethics—both the client's and the social worker's. What has been said about psychotherapy (Kleinsasser & Morton, 1968) applies also to social work: the practitioner's exemplary conduct serves to protect the client when he is in a vulnerable position, and it provides "the client with a concrete experience of an intrinsically moral relationship with another human being," thus to effect "an intricate, often delicate, balance of clinical and ethical values [p. 2]," Kleinsasser and Morton have insisted that these effects are inseparable. One of the most telling media for representing the social worker's intrinsically moral relationship with the client is his express or implied concern about third parties and their interests.

The social worker's ethical liability to third parties is analogous to the accountant's liability to third parties, although their professional responsibilities are not comparable in all respects. The concept employed in relation to accounting certainly provides a serviceable means of illuminating the social worker's ethical responsibility. The Council of The Institute of Chartered Accountants in England and Wales (1965), in an interpretation of accountants' liability for negligence according to the decision of the House of Lords in *Hedley Byrne and Co., Ltd.* v. *Heller and Partners Ltd.*, has defined third-party liability in a manner that makes evident its relevance to social work ethics and its applicability to the social worker's ethical responsibility to persons other than his clients:

> Accountants may now be held in law to owe a duty of care to persons other than those with whom they are in a contractual or fiduciary relationship and may be liable to neglect of that duty if, but only if, they know or ought to know that a financial report, account or statement prepared by them has been prepared for a specific purpose or transaction, will be shown to a particular person or class of persons, and may be relied on by that person or class of persons in that particular connection [p. 164].

We are, of course, not concerned here with the legal technicalities of negligence or legal enforceability for, as the Council (pp. 163–164) itself recognized, the responsibility to third parties has always been acknowledged, "even if it was hitherto considered to be unenforceable in law." Nor is the prospect of a financial or other loss for third parties as a consequence of "reliance on the professional skill and judgement" of practitioners an issue because the primary concern here is the ethical duty owed to persons other than the social worker's client, enforceable or not. Additional subtleties must be considered that affect whether the social worker owes any ethical duty to third parties at all, let alone what kind and with what consideration for his client.

Third parties figure in the ethics of social workers,

despite the primary duties that social workers owe their clients, to the following extent:

1. Third parties may become inadvertent victims of the social work service situation and of the social worker's practice in it.
2. The interests of third parties are affected by the social work service situation and the social worker's practice in it.
3. Third parties have arranged for or initiated service to the social worker's client and are owed specifiable duties because they have done so or because of the way in which they have done so.
4. The intervention or collaboration of third parties is required for the service to be rendered to the social worker's client.
5. Third parties have a legitimate interest in or concern for the social worker's client and the effects of the social worker's service on him.

Social work is a *social* profession in that it is essentially concerned about and is addressed to the client's relation to his social environment (Levy, 1974d). The effect of the social worker's clients on others and of others on them are not merely taken into account by the social worker; they inevitably become a critical dimension of the social worker's practice. This is not a matter of incidental courtesy and foresight but of functional definition. It is a major premise of social work practice. Third parties are an important component of the client's social environment. All that varies is *how* third parties figure in that environment and the specific ethical duties that the social worker owes them as a result.

Responsibility to third parties is essential in social work. There are times and circumstances in fact when social workers consider themselves primarily responsible to third parties although engaged in service to their clients. As

Malmquist (1965) put it in a more general connection:

> Staff members may believe that their main duty is to the community. A similar situation exists in colleges where the therapist is faced with a choice of responsibility to students, to parents or to administration . . . one wonders about the adequacy of evaluations and treatment when the child and parents become aware of the therapist's main loyalties. No such conflict results when the best interests of the community and child coincide, but in practice different emphases in application and goals occur [pp. 788–789].

The social worker's ethical responsibility to his employing institution and the community at large is to be considered in greater detail below, but Malmquist's statement does reflect the essence of the social worker's responsibility to third parties and the conflict that may arise between their interests and those of the client. The social worker's problem is to be duly responsive to his ethical duty to third parties without neglecting his ethical duty to his client.

Extreme loyalty to the client, on the other hand, may result in the neglect of others who may be adversely affected by the client or by what transpires between the client and the social worker. Excessive alignment with the client at the expense of third parties is quite possible, especially, for example, when the social worker is prematurely prone to view the client's parent or spouse as the "enemy" or as the cause of the client's troubled state or deprivation. The social worker's perception may even be accurate. Often it is not, however, because his concentration on the client subjects him to the risk of a biased or unbalanced appraisal of the client's situation. But even if his perception is accurate, the danger from an ethical point of view is that the worker may be more prone to attack the parent or spouse than to assist the client in coping productively with the parent or spouse.

The way the issue was posed for therapy by Grosser

and Paul (1964) is fairly descriptive of what often happens in social work practice:

> The patient is the primary concern of the therapist and the contract is with him; the other family members are, from the point of view of traditional therapeutic technique, a secondary concern whose adjustment problems are not regarded as part of the therapeutic contract. The question therefore arises in conjoint patient-family therapy: "Whose interest is the therapist ethically bound to serve, especially when confronted with issues of intramarital conflict [p. 878]?"

Despite the social worker's gratification about a child's emancipation—perhaps on the social worker's provocation —the child's action may have devastating effects on family members, on the child's relationship to them, and not inconceivably on the child himself. The worker must therefore give some thought to obligations he may have to the family because of why and how the child came to the worker's attention and what is going on in the family.

On the other hand, the right of the child's parents or guardian to share knowledge the social worker acquires through his relationship with the child (when this right can be ascertained, as it sometimes is—ostensibly to make possible provisions that may be necessary for the child's welfare) may be satisfied without paying sufficient attention to the child's right to some privacy. But the social worker cannot readily or arbitrarily deny such a right of the parents or guardian without some doubt about his ethics. At the very least, since children do not normally come to social workers as "autonomous persons in need of help," the issue ought to give the social worker some pause. "The existence of any third party in the relationship poses very real difficulties for any practitioner of a profession [Hall, 1961, p. 111]." Or it ought to.

Certainly when the aid of third parties is enlisted in behalf of clients, the social worker incurs some ethical responsibility to them, depending on the investment of time, energy, or anything else of value to them that they are called on to make and the risks they may be exposed to in the process. They may incur costs (for which the social worker ought to prepare them) or they may be expected to reveal information about themselves that they prefer not to share with anyone else, including the client. Parents who have abused their children or offended sexual norms are examples of third parties at risk to whom social workers may owe particular duty in this connection.

The suggestion is not that, even if the social worker has recruited the efforts of third parties, he should connive at acts of theirs that may place his client in ascertainable jeopardy. But neither can it be suggested that third parties should be inveigled into the service of the social worker's client only to be unceremoniously penalized for their pains. The hazards of ill-considered ethics are only dramatized when such persons are subjected to the social worker's scrutiny against their will, as they may be when they are abusive parents, foster parents, and collaterals in investigative procedures affecting recipients of public assistance.

Just as the social worker must contemplate the consequences for clients of his ministrations as a matter of ethical responsibility, so the consequences for third parties of his practices in relation to them merit consideration. In his compulsion to be honest and candid with third parties, for example—assuming that none of the client's interests will be neglected nor his rights jeopardized—a social worker may bare the lurid details of the client's case without anticipating the effects of those details on the third parties. Such an undisciplined account may well open what Dean (1963), discussing the sharing of psychiatric reports with laymen, described as a Pandora's box. Third parties may misread, misinterpret, or overreact to the account, with possibly shattering effects. Even honesty and candor must be sensitively weighed as far as third parties are concerned, not simply in terms of the effects on the client but in terms of the effects on the third parties themselves.

Some of the dilemmas the social worker faces when considering his ethical responsibility toward third parties are not easily resolved. The responsibility he feels toward his client, and perhaps others as well, often makes these dilemmas especially knotty. Nor is his conviction about his primary as well as ultimate responsibility to the client he is committed and even contracted to serve enough to exempt him from his ethical liability to third parties. That too is a part of social work ethics.

Chapter 13

SOCIAL WORK ETHICS: SOCIETY

The ethics of the social worker includes responsibility to the society around him, not merely as a generic expectation attributable to any red-blooded citizen, but as a function of his status as a social worker. The social worker is expected, as a matter of definition, to do something about conditions in his community, particularly the conditions of its persons in need.

Again, as a *social* profession, social work has long been regarded—and its practitioners tend to regard themselves —as society's cooking spoon. This is not the exclusive province of social workers, but it is in considerable degree peculiar to them. They have appointed themselves, and others have looked to them (not always without exasperation, if not a jaundiced eye) as keepers of "social goals" and "society's values" (e.g., Bartlett, 1958a, b; Boehm, 1958). True, teachers and lawyers have claimed a similar function, but largely as preservers of society rather than as catalytic agents for its modification.[1]

Other human service professions have, of course, also assumed responsibility for societal change in recent years as they, along with others, have reacted with impatience to the slow strides of social progress and have developed conviction about the need for institutional and systemic change. As Felix (1964) put it in relation to psychiatry:

> Tomorrow's psychiatrist will be, as is his counterpart today, one of the gatekeepers of his community, in company with those others who concern themselves with the nature, direction and quality of society in that place. He must be prepared to participate actively and selflessly, as a citizen, as a neighbor, as a person, in matters of concern to the community [p. 322].

Yesterday's social worker was of a similar mind, although he was hardly inclined to man battlements in the struggle for social change.[2] This is not to say that modern social workers are uniformly predisposed to radical social surgery. On the contrary, the social work profession has been censured for according less priority and aggressive attention to institutional and societal change than to its clinical preoccupations and has been urged to change its ways (see Brager, 1967; Cloward & Elman, 1966; National Association of Social Workers, 1969; Rein, 1970). (Other professions have been taken to task on similar grounds: e.g., Berton, 1965.)

[1] Compare, for example, the characterization of the legal profession as "conservative," despite the accreditation of its efforts at social change, in Blaustein, Porter, & Duncan (1954, p. 34).

[2] For a recent discussion of an illustrious example, Jane Addams, see Katz (1975).

Nevertheless, as idealized at least, the social work profession is supposed to stir up the status quo to the extent that people are disadvantaged and deprived and social, economic, and physical conditions are not conducive to their maximal welfare and well-being. As an editorial in the journal of the National Association of Social Workers stated a number of years ago:

> For some time it has been apparent that our technical knowledge and skill (in social work as well as the medical, physical and technological sciences) have far exceeded our social inventiveness. . . . What should be the next steps for social work and social welfare? First, plans must be drawn which will translate our therapeutic experience with individuals and families into coherent programs for dealing with large groups affected by the major social difficulties—disorganization, dependency, dislocation, and disability. The second step is to develop strategies to execute these plans which take into account the contradictory forces, power structures, and interests that make up our nation ["Guest Editorial," p. 2].

This motif is not limited to the era of social revolution that presumably characterized the United States and other countries during the 1960s but actually centered on a few radical movements. These movements did have some impact, but relatively little and not particularly enduring. The revolutionary zeal seems to have lingered longer with the social work profession than with the citizenry at large. And it did begin rather early, with a hint of militancy, to cast the social work profession as either a protagonist for societal underdogs or as an adversary of an otherwise intractable society. The very title of a vintage article by Youngdahl (1947) conveys this: "Social Workers—Stand Up and Be Counted."[3]

---

[3]The history of this trend has been briefly recapitulated in Levy (1963a). It would seem that the grapes of the professional wrath that has been directed against the social work profession, particularly by social

This view of the social work profession's responsibility has been accorded sanction by its professional association, as indicated in the preface to an official policy statement of the National Association of Social Workers (1963):

> These public social policy statements translate into goals for action one of the basic purposes of the National Association of Social Workers described in the bylaws as ". . . to further the broad objective of improving conditions of life in our democratic society through utilization of the professional knowledge and skills of social work . . . to provide opportunity for the social work profession to work in unity toward alleviating or preventing sources of deprivation, distress and strain susceptible of being influenced by social work methods and by social action [p. 3]."

However the issue of practice responsibility is resolved, the nature of the social worker's work and the opportunities made possible by it dictate ethical responsibility beyond the boundaries of his relationship to his client, although that responsibility may be precipitated by what emerges within its boundaries.

Whether as pleader of the cause of individuals and groups or as protagonist of legislative and policy change, the social worker's role and his responsibility for action within it are shaped by and stem from his professional social work responsibility.[4] This both limits and extends his role, but ethically speaking he is never free of it. What he does with the role on the job—that is, in his relationship with his client—requires some correlation with his responsibility in the job. The sky is the virtual limit when the social worker works for an agency whose avowed and chartered mission is the espousal of the social causes of its clientele. The social worker's activity on the job, however, must bear

workers, should have ripened sufficiently long before this to fall off the vine or simply wither and die, but instead they go on fermenting in the social work literature.

[4]This part of the discussion is drawn freely from Levy (1974a).

some relationship to his job description. For the private practitioner, the limits and opportunities are related to his clients' needs and rights as members of classes of persons whose lot might be affected favorably by systematic and informed social action.

Within the framework of his employing agency's function or his specific professional responsibility, the social worker's focus in this context is not simply particular benefits for his clients but institutional and societal conditions that affect his clients and others like them. As unwieldy as this may be—and often, as fruitless as it may be—the social worker's aim is in some way, usually in concert with others, to affect the society and its institutions so that persons and groups like his clients will be more equitably dealt with and receive a greater share of society's resources.[5] His objective is to change society and its institutions in ways that will benefit his clients too.

The social worker owes skilled efforts to ensure equal opportunities and protections to all persons within the framework of formal and informal institutions and practices, and of voluntary as well as governmental institutions and procedures. The worker is professionally obliged to devote himself to effecting for persons at the lowest socioeconomic rungs (if their being there subjects them to social neglect) all the rights and entitlements that are legally and socially available to others. Barry (1965) has described this modest goal as "procedural fairness": "To say that a procedure is being fairly operated is to say that the formalities which define the procedure have been correctly adhered to [p. 97]."

The social worker's mission is to see to it that these formalities are in fact adhered to, that such obligations as

---

[5]Some of the complications the social worker faces in his attempts to effect social change, whether alone or in collaboration with others, are suggested in Levy (1973c).

may be owed to people under law, governmental policy, and agency policies are enforced. All modes of obligation and expectation are encompassed in this mission including those governed by private contracts and social policies. The social worker who detects the failure of government, courts, agencies, corporations, businesses, and individuals (slumlords, for example) to meet their obligations to clients and disadvantaged groups must be moved to act on the latter's behalf until they are met.

The simple fulfillment of such obligations is often insufficient, however. Sometimes ostensible beneficiaries are not in a position to benefit equally from them in the first place. These obligations may have to be reconstituted to compensate for inequalities between affected parties or to equalize the circumstances under which the obligations operate—to make the parties more equal than they might tend to be without some adjustment in or redefinition of the obligations.

Equal provisions and equal opportunities, although ensured by government and agencies, are not always sufficient for persons and groups in limited or deprived circumstances. Special provisions must be made to provide them with opportunities that are truly more equal. The social worker must do what he can to make certain that "some evaluations in terms of 'fairness' dig a little deeper and ask whether the background conditions are satisfactory," a test that Barry (1965, pp. 97–98) describes as "background fairness." "Equal protections" often neglect the deficiencies and miseries that prevent people from full recourse to purportedly universal provisions (cf. "Developments in the Law"). The guarantees of bail and legal counsel hardly guarantee access to these provisions, let alone their adequacy for abandoned or impoverished persons.

The ethics of the social worker demands efforts on his part to effect equity and to compensate for conditions and circumstances that prevent persons and groups from having equal access to procedures, goods, and services which supposedly are available to them. If it is an agency's function to provide marriage counseling, but the agency strictly construes marital status in legal terms, then the social worker may have to make representations within or to the agency to relax its definition and permit an unmarried couple access to the service if they wish it. If government funds are legislated for certain programs but the restrictions have the effect of excluding particular neighborhoods or agencies, then the social worker may have to try to change the situation. If election provisions limit the opportunity for adequate representation on community-action boards or if civil service examinations are timed or located to rule out Blacks or Jews, then active pleading or protest by the social worker may be called for. Any operational restrictions of otherwise equal protection-oriented legislation and policies may require the social worker's intervention.

Beyond that, the social worker may find it necessary to act to ensure the selective consideration of the needs of deprived groups and the institution of differential provisions for them in light of their present condition and past deprivations. In such a case, it is not merely a matter of ensuring equal access to the goods and services made available by law and agency policy but of making preferential provisions available to specific persons and groups. The social worker addresses his efforts in response to the requirement "that a person [or group] who has been deprived of his just share . . . be appropriately compensated for his deprivation [Fried, 1970, p. 220]." The intent is to redress the effects, among other things, "of past racial discrimination by giving special treatment to particular racial groups in such fields as education, public employment and housing ["Developments in the Law," p. 1104]." In response to this ethical responsibility in general, the social worker would make deliberate attempts to effect *differential* opportunities to compensate certain groups for past inequities and to accelerate their socioeconomic rise.

The social worker as an agency representative can, in complete ethical harmony with his job description, engage in action to effect social change of these types when that change coincides with the agency's avowed mission. He may have a full caseload of children placed in foster homes, for example, and pursue separately a particular course of action or influence affecting the welfare of children in general.

As a social worker identified with the goals and responsibilities of the social work profession, he may also act against more general and pervasive social problems and in behalf of more widespread social needs. His professional value orientation would make it incumbent upon him, as a member of the social work profession, to do his share to improve the society and the fate of its members. But even as a private citizen the social worker, because he is a social worker and is therefore informed about the plight of persons and groups and their needs, should feel committed to action for changes that will help to meet people's needs, improve social conditions, and correct legal and social inequities (Levy, 1965b).

The social worker, in other words, is responsible for the consequences of the knowledge at his disposal, and his background as well as his practice experience place such knowledge at his disposal. He is supposed to know something about the conditions and circumstances of people. He has firsthand contact with them and is in a position to know what they need and what the society must do in order for them to get it. He is expected to feel with them in their difficulties and deprivations. He is ethically required to do something with and about what he knows. This includes anticipating effects of current policies and events and urg-

ing plans for coping with them on community and government leadership (Levy, 1971).

Another, perhaps more innocuous aspect of the social
worker's ethical responsibility to and for his society concerns his conduct, behavior, and associations in relation to
it. As a social worker, he must not forget that he speaks and
acts with whatever influence and authority may be associated with his profession. There are obviously many social
circles in which this statement would be more of an apolo-
getic acknowledgment than an awe-inspiring one. But in
some circles, the fact that he is a social worker might matter, and he must give some thought to the difference this
fact might make and to the consequences for the standing
of social work and social workers in the community. Although social workers may not be inspiring role models in
some quarters, what they do or do not do—including their
stances on social issues—might very well be bases for judgments about their profession and its practitioners.

Positively or negatively, the social worker's professional status accrues to him a degree of potential power or
influence, and he is ethically responsible for the use he
makes or does not make of that power or influence. A
prophecy, a judgment, a forecast, or a testimonial that
might reasonably be regarded by others as a function of
professional wisdom, bias, or experience must be pro-
nounced in measured and discriminating tones. The social
worker must exercise great care and responsibility in the
manner in which, as a social worker, he presents himself to,
deals with, and helps the community of which he is a part.
He must exercise scrupulous restraint in his judgments and
in his behavior and associations. What he chooses to do as
well as not do affects judgments about his profession in
relation to society.

As a member of a social profession, the social worker
is expected to be just in all his dealings and to do what he
can to see justice done. Despite his loyalty to his clients and

his zeal for social improvements in their interest, the reasonable interests and welfare of others merit his ethical consideration.[6] The social worker owes it to himself, his profession, and society to be guided by a social orientation. Aside from being alert to social problems and assuming his share of responsibility for solving them, he carries affirmative responsibility to advance the well-being and interests of society as a whole. He must avoid intruding on any measure—including the increase and availability of competent professional manpower and of social, medical, and other services—that will best serve the society and its members. He must be ready to lend initiative and leadership to the task of improving the collective lot of man, particularly in matters related to his field of competence.

The social worker must uphold the community's laws and help make them work toward a healthy and productive community and citizenry, even as he seeks to change them so that they work better than they do. As is sometimes stated in professional codes of ethics, the social worker's principal objectives are to render service to humanity with full respect for the dignity of human beings and to respect the social ideals honored by his profession. This implies an abiding concern for the prevention as well as treatment of social ills and for the nurture and conservation of available resources and the optimal use of them for the general welfare. His knowledge and skill should be used, insofar as possible, for the common weal.

Society is very much an abstraction as far as the social work function is concerned. But the ethics of the social worker in relation to society emphasizes responsibilities and expectations that extend beyond his work with clients, without infringing on society—and them.

[6]Compare the principles of justice that are the foundation for Rawls's (1971, pp. 60–62) theory of justice.

Chapter 14

SOCIAL WORK ETHICS: EMPLOYERS

It seems unnecessary to say much about the social worker's ethical responsibility to his employer or employers. The mutual duties between employer and employee have been prescribed for centuries. Common law provisions, moreover, were pretty much ethically founded, emphasizing as they did the obligations of master and servant to each other. The conception of mutuality in the eighteenth century was vastly different from the modern conception, but both master and servant were held to a fairly demanding standard of morality in relation to one another. As indicated in Blackstone's "Commentaries" (Ehrlich, 1959) slavery was verboten as an excessively unilateral arrangement and one that was "repugnant to reason, and the principles of natural law [p. 70]." The responsibility of employer to employee and employee to employer was regarded as so imperative, in fact, that Blackstone listed the relationship between them first among "the three great relations in private life," *before* those of husband and wife and parent and child. In his time, as now, the mutual loyalty of employer and employee was a minimal expectation. As the "Commentaries" phrased it:

> A master . . . may justify an assault in defense of his servant, and a servant in defense of his master; the master, because he has an interest in his servant, not to be deprived of his service; the servant, because it is part of his duty, for which he received his wages, to stand by and defend his master [p. 75].

And of course the master was held answerable for the act of his servant in the line of duty to his master and was liable to third parties for the servant's negligence or wrongdoing while attending to his duties to his master, or as a consequence of his attention to those duties.

In other words, the rules and norms affecting the ethical responsibility of social workers to their employers would seem evident enough, on the basis of general and enduring principles affecting employers and employees, not to require extensive consideration. At the same time, the issues affecting the social worker's ethical responsibility toward his employer or employing agency are sufficiently complex to merit at least some delineation.

The first question to be tackled is who the social worker's employer is. Often it is an agency, an organization, or an institution, but because ethics can hardly be applied to inanimate objects or abstract entities, this means that the social worker is accountable for both his ethics and his professional performance to those persons or groups who, acting for the agency, organization, or institution, have engaged his services and have the authority to terminate them. These persons or groups may be professional colleagues who are entrusted with administrative and supervisory responsibilities, including some kind of jurisdiction over the social worker, or groups of volunteers who act as trustees of the community in making policies and overseeing the operation of the agency, organization, or institution. Generally it is a colleague, who may or may not be another social worker, who implements the volunteers' intentions and is therefore the person who deals with the social worker and with whom the social worker deals. If the social worker is an administrator himself, then he is held to account directly to the volunteers. In any of these arrangements, the basis for mutual expectations may be an explicit contract; the general customs and usage of the social work profession and social welfare field; or the policy, practices, and procedures of the employers to the extent that they represent the mutual understanding of employer and employee.

When the employer is a business, a governmental agency, or a military unit, policies, laws, or administrative procedures govern the social worker's ethics—as well as the employer's ethics in relation to him—which is then monitored by other staff, perhaps but not necessarily other social workers.

Since the social worker's work, directly or indirectly, is usually addressed to clients, it may seem that his ethical responsibility to his employer is purely incidental to his primary responsibility to his clients. As it was put in relation to the rehabilitation counselor (Geist, G. O., Curin, S., Prestridge, R., & Schleb, G., 1973) "the agency should be little more than a place . . . to hang his hat [p. 17]." There is no doubt that employing agencies sometimes devote more energy to and hence apply more pressure on social workers in the cause of their own survival than in the service of their clienteles, but the following view, which has been expressed with regard to the relationship between the rehabilitation counselor and his employing agency and is often entertained in relation to social workers and their employers, may be insufficiently responsive to the practitioner's responsibility to his employer:

One of the main functions of agencies is to serve the counselor in his attempts to serve the client. Ideally, an agency
is organized and established to meet the perceived needs of
a client population. The means for doing this is to provide
administrative, secretarial, professional, and other services,
the purpose of which is to facilitate essential client services.
The agency is established to facilitate the professional
rehabilitation counselor's effective functioning with a client
[Geist et al., 1973, p. 17].

This sounds plausible enough, especially if the agency's
purpose is to provide the kind of service that the practitioner is equipped and employed to give. But there are
ethical strictures with respect not only to what the employing agency does for the social worker but to what the social
worker does for the employing agency. Not that right or
wrong the agency is always right; however, devotion and
loyalty applies to the social worker's employing agency as
much as it does to the social worker's client.

That this is an essential ethical principle may be reflected in the recognition of the fact that sometimes the
client *is* the employer. This is certainly true when the social
worker is a private practitioner. This evokes a kind of ethical syllogism for if the social worker owes devotion and
loyalty to his client, and his client is his employer, then he
owes devotion and loyalty to his employer. When he is
employed to provide social work service to the employer's
clientele, we have that peculiar kind of intricacy that has
long intrigued literary critics who have tried to estimate
how the performance of an Elizabethan boy who played a
girl disguised as a boy in Shakespeare's plays was appraised. These situations are indeed wheels within wheels,
but they require ethical fathoming if the social worker is to
be able to resolve conflicts between his employer and his
client and to act ethically in relation to both. For the fact
remains that, simply on contractual grounds, no matter

how informal the employment agreement between the social worker and his employer, when the employer is an institution "the authority of the institution must be upheld and respected at the same time that the welfare of the client is advanced." Unfortunately, as Hackbush (1948) admonished, "These two things are not always compatible [p. 86]."

The ethics of the social worker in relation to a client who engages his service for a stipulated fee is not appreciably different from the ethics of the social worker in relation to clients in general, whether they pay or not. Because of the professional base and implications of social work service, the identification of the social worker-client relationship as an employee-employer relationship is distasteful to social workers. And yet some of the ethical duties owed to clients are a function of the employer-employee implications of the social worker-client relationship. This is in part the justification for using the term client: the word carries the connotation of practitioner independence, initiative, and judgment without losing sight of the autonomy and jurisdiction of the beneficiary of the social worker's service, much as it does in relation to law and accounting. These connotations are not associated with the term "patient."

Though not germane here, an agency (in other words, the persons who carry authority and responsibility in and for the agency) that employs the social worker in any capacity also owes ethical responsibility to the social worker. But to concentrate on the main purpose here, the social worker owes specific ethical responsibilities to his employing agency. Foremost among these is the responsibility to act for, and represent the agency loyally and well—not without some thought to, and responsibility for inequities and injustices that the agency may inflict on others, but unequivocally nonetheless—unless or until he severs his relationship with the agency. This is not a matter of blind and rigid loyalty without regard for its consequences, but a contracted obligation in the sense that if the social worker works for an agency, he works for and not against it. Second, the social worker does what the agency employs him to do in fulfilling the agency's declared purpose and service function, not something else.

An agency whose existence is in danger because of a proposed community organization plan is entitled to defense by the social worker who is assigned to represent it and make its pleadings in the community organization, even if the social worker doubts the validity of its perpetuation, at least in its contemporary form. Is this dishonest or opportunistic? It seems so, but it need not be if the worker simply responds to his charge—the communication of his agency's position. This does not prevent him from exercising his initiative and using his opportunities within the agency to urge the agency to reconsider its purpose, function, and approach to service, if indeed he is convinced that the agency's practices and policies require reconsideration or modification in the interest of sound community planning and the most effective use of available community resources.

Consider the alternative. Picture the social worker, sent to present his agency's point of view and expected to represent it well, who proceeds to scuttle his own agency, even out of the idealistic illusion that he owes transcendent loyalty to the "big picture." There are places and opportunities to advance the larger collective interests of the community, but the question is: Is this the place and opportunity and is it appropriate for the social worker to respond in these terms in this setting?

Lest this appear to be an unduly restricting principle and one totally incompatible with the social worker's responsibility to his clients, who in this case are also the employing agency's clients, a few of the opportunities available to the social worker to act on his clients' behalf will be briefly reviewed.

In the very implementation of his agency function—
and this is completely consistent with the principle of devotion and loyalty to his employing agency—the social worker
can, ethically, represent to the agency, on his own initiative,
the interests and concerns of his clients. On the basis of
experience and practice, he gathers judgments about the
needs, interests, preferences, or views of agency clients.
When these judgments appear to require an institutional
response, the social worker can channel them into the
agency's administrative process in an attempt to effect
changes that will benefit the agency's clients (Levy, 1970).

If the social worker succeeds in precipitating agency
reform, he is doing so within the administrative structure
of which he himself is a part and is using legitimate and
sanctioned agency processes—though the agency's administrators or governing group may be disquieted by his actions. The actions are not unethical at any rate. And as far
as the clients are concerned, they are ethical, and to omit
them might not be. Therefore, in effect the social worker's
initiative in representing the clients' needs as well as views
to the agency and in trying to influence agency change in
a way that would accommodate them, is implementing
agency-assigned responsibility to the extent that, through
administrative or social work practice, he is employed to
render service to clients.

The social worker may also use his opportunities and
influence to try to effect a role for clients in the formulation
of agency policy and in agency decision-making, either
through the informality of an advisory committee or
through the formality of official representation and voting
power in the governing groups. This is not unethical from
the viewpoint of the social worker's ethical responsibility to
his employing agency to the extent that he is directly or
indirectly responsible for service to, and the self-determination of clients—depending on whether he is an administrator, a practitioner, or a combination of both—and to the

extent that the authoritative voice and participation of clients might lead to improved service for them.

It would not even be unethical for the social worker, in relation to his employing agency, to advise his clients of the limits of their influence if they operate within the boundaries of agency-sanctioned participation because frequently this proves to be a form of co-optation. This may be a simple fact, and his ethical responsibility to his clients requires the truth. Agency-employed social workers being no less bound by social work ethics than private practitioners, the social worker would be expected to be truthful—not by engaging in an open alignment with clients against the agency but by addressing realistically the limits that clients face, and clarifying the issues they must resolve in attempting to realize their own aspirations which the social worker also helps them to define. In doing these things the social worker is not only carrying out responsibility to clients, but also fulfilling his agency function. This, too, is part of his ethical responsibility to his employer.

Less clear, ethically, is the validation of the social worker's acts on behalf of his clients (which may be in conflict with the agency's policies) on the basis of the social work code of ethics. As Geist et al. (1973, p. 20) suggest, there may be good and sufficient reason for the profession to police the ethics of its members, but agency requirements and the profession's code do not invariably coincide. Whatever influence and sanctions the profession may be able to exert on agencies, perhaps to discourage social workers from taking professional employment with them and perhaps even to censure or excommunicate them when they act in consonance with agency expectations and in dissonance with the profession's code, it is the agency's policies that the social worker has committed himself to when he accepts employment with the agency, and deviating from its policies without legitimating provisions must be regarded as unethical until the policies change. And the social worker may well make it his business to change them —sometimes under the impetus of his professional ethics.

With a modicum of ingenuity, the social worker may find that the practices or procedures of his employing agency violate its own policies or the law or norms on which they are based. In such a case, it is not a question of supporting a policy until a change in it can be attempted, but of identifying a deviation from an existing policy and insisting on adherence to it to serve the interests of clients and safeguard their entitlements. This is, of course, not only not unethical: to fail to respond to and cope with such a departure would be unethical, in relation to both clients and the agency. But the ingenuity that is needed relates to the capacity to perceive a disparity between the agency's policies (or norms, espoused values, law, or whatever) and its or its staff's actions.

A good—or actually bad—example is that supreme indignity of indignities, the "midnight raid," which is in somewhat unfavorable repute at the moment but lurks in the wings to spring out anew, perhaps in less manifestly illegal form, at the slightest hint of vulnerability in the public assistance program—and nothing contributes more to such vulnerability than a tight economy and rising welfare rolls.

The term midnight raid is defined by the National Association of Social Workers (*Midnight Raids*) as a "surprise [a rather ironic description, is it not?] visit [to a welfare client] at an unconventional hour (*NASW News*, November, 1964)," entry being easily gained by the duress implicit in the client's concern about losing the financial assistance he has been getting and may desperately need.

> The question of whether such raids infringe the constitutional rights of citizens receiving public assistance is being pursued through legal channels. For the individual social worker, however, the "midnight raid" poses other serious problems. He may be charged with unethical behavior if he

is accused of being party to such an action or he may be penalized if he refuses to be a participant [*Midnight Raids*].

Whether the social worker will resist participation (as some social workers have) or not is a matter of ethics as well as of law. But the choice is ethically clearer if the social worker can resort to an internal inconsistency between the agency's action and its policies or values. The social worker is only doing his job—loyally and proficiently—if he calls the contradiction to the agency's attention.

Nor need the action be so disastrous or so offensive to either the social worker's or the client's integrity and dignity. Agencies are not invariably disinclined to decide on a course of action that clearly conflicts with their own avowed purposes. An example is the establishment of membership or eligibility regulations or other procedures that tend to exclude the very clients an agency was created to serve, or certainly to discourage or impede their access to the agency —sometimes with the specific though obscured intention of discriminative selection of clientele. A social worker who neglects to point out the inconsistency, though he perceives it, is not ethical—either in relation to the affected clients or in relation to the agency. He owes the agency the truth just as much as he owes it to his clients, and with vigor when an injustice or inequity, such as unjustly depriving a client of a service that he needs, is likely to result.

More affirmatively, the social worker is bound to represent and reflect in all his actions as a member of the agency's staff those values the agency may be associated with (a sectarian agency, for example) and to demand the same of others who represent and work for the agency. In these instances, the ethical social worker's position is stronger and more obligatory because he is only doing and expecting of the agency's staff and leadership that which they have undertaken to do in the first place. His own ethics in relation to the agency reinforces the agency's ethics in relation to its own purposes and the values with which the agency has identified itself.

The need for ethical clarity becomes especially impressive when one considers the corrupting pressure that the agency sometimes exerts on the social worker. When the agency is subject to an elusive internal contradiction, the social worker can act with the strength of the conviction that if the agency is or has ever been true to its own service convictions, it can be moved to overcome its waywardness. If logic will not do it, perhaps conscience will.

But there are times when the agency's action is not inconsistent with its own purposes, but the social worker perceives it as a violation of the professional ethics to which he feels committed. This manifestation could be an occasional or a recurring one. Either way, the social worker feels pressed to make his ethical choice or to survive with his internal dissonance. Whether or not he acts in response to what he regards as his ethical responsibility to the agency and to those who are affected by its actions, he is apt to feel conflict. The more a "captive" of his agency he feels, the more conflict he feels and thus the less ethical:

> When a member of one of the "free" professions becomes an employee of a bureaucratic organization, the organization often supersedes the ultimate control normally invested in his professional colleagues, and the professional thus becomes a "captive." The captivity of employment may then create conflicts for the professional caught between the value systems of his profession and those of the organization to which he submits [Daniels, 1969, p. 255].

To lapse into the relatively mundane (but without dwelling on it) the social worker's ethics in relation to his employer—whether client, industry (social workers do function in industry), government, agency, institution, or organization—requires scrupulous use of and accounting for the employer's funds and resources; prompt and efficient fulfillment of administrative, practice, fiscal, statistical, and other procedures; timely and effective communication of data concerning clientele, public reactions, community attitudes, and other matters that bear on the employer's purposes and functions and might affect the employer's plans, decisions, and actions; cooperation and collaboration in evaluation procedures; and attempted implementation of innovations and changes.

The ethical principles discussed in this chapter do not exhaust the substance of the social worker's ethical responsibility to his employer, but they do suggest the breadth of its range. Although they do not make social work ethics less difficult, they do indicate why social work ethics is so necessary.

Chapter 15

SOCIAL WORK ETHICS: COLLEAGUES

The final category of social work ethics to be considered poses peculiar difficulties. Colleague is an inherently complex and diffuse concept. Its very definition indicates as much. For example, the unabridged *Random House Dictionary of the English Language* defines a colleague as "an associate in any office, profession, work, or the like" and stops after one illustration. And if the definition were not so elastic, it would have to be stretched for the purposes of this discussion.

The ethical considerations affecting the social worker's relationship to his colleagues are broad in scope, diverse in their operation, varied in their intensity, and assorted in their application to social workers' practices and relationships in their professional capacity and career peregrinations. It is hard to see how a common or a generic enough foundation can be found for intelligible discussion of the social worker's ethics in relation to his colleagues. And yet there is a thread of universality to the ethical principles that link the social worker to the diversity of colleagues to whom he may be said to have some ethical responsibility and to the diversity of settings and circumstances in which he encounters them, sometimes with assigned professional responsibility to them or authority over them and sometimes with no explicit or enforceable expectations in relation to them. Some colleagues to whom the social worker may be said to have ethical responsibility he never even sees.

For a better appreciation of the nuances of this discussion, the following typology of the social worker's colleagues is offered:

1. Members of the social work profession.
2. Co-workers in the social worker's agency, office, and so on who are also social workers.
3. Co-workers in the social worker's agency or office who are not social workers.
4. The social worker's subordinates or supervisees.
5. The social worker's administrative superiors.
6. Students in training. (In social work education, the social worker who supervises students of graduate schools of social work placed in social agencies for a kind of extensive and intensive internship is described as either a supervisor or a field instructor.)
7. Candidates for jobs that will make them the social worker's peers or subordinates.
8. The social worker's prospective employers, whether social workers or not.

The operation of the ethical principles to be considered will vary according to the classification of the colleagues to whom they apply or whom they affect. In general, however, these principles have a distinctive character as compared with the principles applicable to the other categories of ethics discussed in the preceding chapters.

Sir Thomas Lund (1960, p. 1) treated this category of ethical principles as a matter of etiquette, and he regarded deviation from them as a breach of good manners for which only the extreme penalty, and only in carefully regulated professions, might be exclusion from membership in the professional association and, in rare instances, from membership in the profession. This may be more consequential than it sounds because in some professions and in some jurisdictions, either of these fates would mean the deprivation of the legal right or the privilege to practice.[1] Nevertheless, the charge in the event of an offense against such a principle would be based on the practitioner's failure to conform "with the accepted conduct of and traditional behavior of solicitors, who are gentlemen [p.1]," to use Sir Thomas's very British phrase.

This understates the importance of these ethical principles, however, as Pellegrino (1964) has emphasized, and what he says about medicine is equally applicable to social work:

> Ethics, properly speaking, deals with the rightness or wrongness of the physician's actions in the light of principles which arise out of the nature of man as a person. It establishes normative guides which govern specific situations in such a way that the rights of patients are always preserved.
>
> Professional etiquette on the other hand deals with duties arising out of the relations of physicians with each other and out of the dignity of the calling. The public has never found it difficult to understand the truly ethical principles which assure high standards of service and devotion. The proscriptions relating to the conduct of physicians with each

[1]See, for example, Brand (1956) for a review of data on the incidence in the United States of integrated state bar associations, which signifies the inseparability, for the purposes of the franchise to practice law and the rules governing practice, between the existing professional associations and the political structures of a state.

other are less clear to the public who sometimes erroneously interpret them as self-protective devices [p. 111].

Pellegrino goes on to admit that the human rights of patients may not be affected by proscriptions such as the forbidding of advertising, and the splitting of fees, and by departures from prescribed conditions of medical practice, courtesies of consultation, and responsibility for the promotion of public health, although offenses on these counts might impair the dignity of the medical profession. But, he insists, neither medicine nor nursing can neglect principles of professional conduct or of the conduct of professional practitioners, which directly or indirectly affects patients. He attributes similar responsibility to other members of medical care teams, which make it obligatory for all their participants to engage in cooperative activity in behalf of patients and to assume collective responsibility for patients' dignity and rights. This necessitates that they surrender some of their individualism and accept the discipline of a conjoint effort. "The time-honored ethical principles which protect the rights of the patient," he adds, "must remain operative [p. 112]."

In relation to colleagues in the profession at large, the social worker is ethically responsible not only to avoid doing what is "just not done" because of the unsalutary effect it may have on particular practitioners, practitioners in general, or the social work profession as a whole, but also to do affirmatively and responsibly what will redound to the status, standing, productivity, and benefit of colleagues and to the credit of the social work profession.

The social worker is expected to seek opportunities and avail himself of all existing media at his disposal to enrich the fund of social work knowledge and the reservoir of the social work profession's personal, educational, and other resources. He is expected to treat colleagues fairly, both in terms of civility, just rewards, and recognition and

in terms of opportunity for continued development as practitioners. In addition, he is expected to encourage others
to practice ethically and to facilitate their doing so.

Self-centeredness and selfishness in relationships with
colleagues are an ethical abomination; selflessness and self-
sacrifice, the operative norm. The social worker is enjoined
from making progress at the expense of his colleagues'
income, reputation, prospects, and so forth. On the contrary, he is encouraged to help his colleagues and his profession with generous allocations of his resources, time,
talent, and effort by supporting and participating in professional associations and by collaborating in research, training, and other professional endeavors.

To be ethical in relation to colleagues, the social
worker must be discreet in his announcements, advertising,
and use of his name, title, and identification. One offense
to be avoided is that of being self-serving or competitive.
The etiquette of consultation is similarly demanding: it
requires the most scrupulous observance of rules and procedures designed to discourage invidious references to or
implications concerning another practitioner's competence
or service, or pirating of another's position, clients, or staff.
Even distributing reprints and scholarly papers to spread
one's fame or to compete unfairly for employment or other
opportunities is ethically offensive, although one is responsible for sharing his knowledge with colleagues as well as
sustaining the threat of continuity with their work, with due
acknowledgement of their contributions when he uses
them.

The social worker is supposed to exercise restraint
when he differs with a colleague, especially in the presence
of clients. This does not mean he cannot have differences,
but he must be considerate in the manner in which he
expresses them as well as where he expresses them and
when. As a matter of courtesy at least, the social worker is
supposed to talk to his colleague before he talks to the

client. Good taste, tact, and harmony are desiderata. On the other hand, the implication of a combination of colleagues in restraint of professional communication must also be studiously avoided.

Since service to oneself or one's family is frowned on for reasons already discussed, the social worker is expected to resort to other social workers for the social work service that he or his loved ones may need. (It is hardly confidence-inspiring for a social worker to avoid the ministrations of social workers when that is what is needed; yet an occasional worker tends to accord it a low priority or to avoid it altogether. Social workers have even been known to bad-mouth social work as a career choice for family members and friends, which hardly contributes to others' faith in it. This too would have to be appraised as unethical.) Professional courtesy may be extended in such cases, but some thought must be given to deprivations to others as a result.

With respect to colleagues whom the social worker supervises within a bureaucratic structure, a special order of ethics is required. This becomes evident when one considers the relatively disadvantaged position of the supervisee as compared with the supervisor (Levy, 1973b).

1. *The supervisor has administratively assigned and sanctioned authority over the supervisee.* The supervisory relationship is usually a condition of the supervisee's employment: that is, a supervisor is assigned to the supervisee; he is not an optional figure in the supervisee's agency career. Supervisory responsibility is usually defined in terms of control over the supervisee and the supervisee's accountability to the supervisor, although a common implicit or explicit component of that responsibility is the provision of assistance and guidance.

2. *The supervisor mediates the relationship between the su-*

pervisee and the employing agency. Depending on the supervisor's position in the agency hierarchy and the function he performs in it, he represents and interprets the supervisee to those with greater authority and in turn determines whether and how the agency will be represented and interpreted to the supervisee. The higher the supervisor's hierarchical position, of course, the greater his potential influence and control over the supervisee will be.

3. *The supervisor usually plays a role in hiring or firing the supervisee.* The higher the supervisor's hierarchical position in the agency, the greater his immediate jurisdiction over the supervisee's job and the greater his power over the supervisee will be. However, any supervisor has some jurisdiction over his supervisee's job because he is in a position to judge the supervisee's job performance. The more the supervisee needs the job and the less mobile he feels because of his personal or professional limitations or limited job opportunities, the less independent he tends to feel. As Mills (1956) pointed out:

> In almost any job, the employee sells a degree of his independence; his working life is within the domain of others; the level of his skills that are used and the areas in which he may exercise independent decisions are subject to management by others [p. 224].

The supervisor is certainly one of these "others" and often a significant one in the supervisee's life.

4. *The supervisor controls the supervisee's salary increases and promotions to some degree and determines the kinds of entries that will appear in his record.* Although the supervisee's job may not be threatened, his status

and movement in it are likely to be contingent
upon the supervisor's appraisal of his performance no matter how accurate or inaccurate, relevant or irrelevant.

> The comparative intimacy of the supervisory relationship
> and the recognized factors of control in it tend to make it a
> sphere in which one can do, with comparative safety, many
> of the things one might like to do in other relationships in
> which one is held back for one reason or another. . . . It must
> be recognized . . . that it is possible to misuse a situation in
> which there are so many factors favorable to one party in the
> relationship. . . . This inequality is epitomized, so to speak,
> in the supervisor's power to evaluate. This is a power of
> which the supervisee is conscious [Aptekar, 1954, p. 239].

Implicit in the following admonitory statement about
supervisors' authority to grant salary increases is the nature
of the power this kind of authority implies and the possibility of abusing it:

> Authority over the granting of increases is not designed as
> a punitive device for irresponsible use. It is definitely *not* a
> license for a supervisor to penalize an employee without
> fully explaining the reason for the penalty or without an
> opportunity for the employee to present his side of the case
> fully to someone other than the supervisor [United States
> Civil Service Commission, 1965].

5. *Although the supervisor is not inevitably more professionally competent than the supervisee, he almost invariably
   knows more than the supervisee about some things.* To
   the extent that the supervisor knows more than
   does the supervisee, he has power to wield over
   him. If the supervisor is also more experienced in
   and knowledgeable about the supervisee's job,
   his power is increased. Perlman (1967) has alluded to "knowledge and know-how" as a source

of power that certainly affects an uneducated or inexperienced supervisee. The supervisor may not actually possess greater professional wisdom and acumen than the supervisee does, but if the supervisee *believes* he does, the supervisor has power over him. This is understandable because the supervisee reacts to the supervisor "as a symbol of a system and not just a person [Aptekar, 1965, p. 11]."

Even if the supervisee is cynical about the supervisor's professional knowledge, the supervisor, as part of management, is likely to have information to which the supervisee does not have ready access. The supervisor is therefore a conduit of communication and may, if he wishes to achieve some strategic end, parcel out information grudgingly or withhold it altogether. This ability to censor information is a form of managerial power that may be "converted to personal influence [Blau, 1964, pp. 206–207]."

The supervisor's stance of possessing superior knowledge becomes a "manipulative controlling device." Therefore, if the supervisee's judgment differs from his supervisor's, the supervisor may accuse him of being unable to accept supervision (Blau & Scott, 1962). The supervisor may genuinely believe he is right, but his position permits him the unilateral option of deciding that he is, and the insecure or uncertain supervisee has neither the competence nor the choice to doubt him.

6. *The supervisor expects, if not requires, the supervisee to reveal much about himself in the supervisory relationship.* The supervisee exposes himself to the risk of having his revelations used inappropriately or misused, at least in ways that are disadvantageous to him. Although it is not valid to discuss, during supervisory conferences, information that is re-

lated more to the supervisee's private life than to his job performance, this may happen unless the supervisor discourages it. However, even if the discussions in supervisory conferences are relevant to the supervisee's job and germane to the agency's legitimate interest in it, the supervisor is in a position to use or misuse whatever the supervisee reveals. In fact, if the supervisee fails to identify weaknesses and impediments he is aware of in his own performance and development as a practitioner, the supervisor may conclude that he is aborting or hindering his opportunities to receive the supervisor's help and guidance, which are considered legitimate supervisory functions. The supervisor, on the other hand, is not required to reciprocate. He is expected to exercise sufficient control over his conversations with the supervisee to keep the focus of attention on the supervisee and his job unless, in *his* judgment, discussing his own role will implement his supervisory function in relation to the supervisee.

7.   *The supervisor's influence extends beyond the supervisee's tenure on the job.* Judgments about the supervisee's performance in the agency as well as how these judgments are phrased affect the supervisee long afterward. For example, the less accurate or fair the supervisor's evaluation or reference letter is, the more it can unjustly skew the supervisee's future job opportunities.

Reynolds (1942) long ago assembled a set of principles governing the supervisor's responsibility to write reference letters that are timely, current, job-related, and so on. These principles attest to the enduring nature of the supervisor's control over the supervisee's fate and behavior and suggest the relative powerlessness of supervisees who may

find themselves haunted and victimized by written judgments that may not have been or no longer are fair esti-
mates of their capacities, or perhaps are not germane in
substance or interpretation to the purposes for which they
are used. The fact that the supervisee may never have seen
those judgments or had opportunity to refute them only
augments the offense.

The social worker's supervisory practice in an agency
should not be guided any the less by agency values than is
the agency's service to clients. In fact his supervisory practice may serve as a model for supervisees' helping relationships with others and thus inspire ethical practice and the
application of those values that the agency and the social
work profession subscribe to. Ethical principles are, after
all, also values [compare Edel, 1963, chap. 9]. The supervisor's scrupulous regard for the supervisee's welfare and
development stems not only from the definition of the supervisor's function in the agency but also from his ethically-
motivated concern for the supervisee as a human being—
a concern to which the supervisor is committed as a professional social worker.

When the supervisor participates in the process of employing the supervisee and fashioning his job assignment,
he should feel subject to ethical constraints that transcend
his agency responsibility. His ethics demands his unbiased
consideration and a considerate approach when evaluating
the supervisee for the job. The supervisee should be assigned to a job in which he can succeed and to one that is
worthy of him. The supervisor owes the supervisee a good
start, and it is his ethical obligation to provide whatever the
supervisee needs to do his job. Even if the supervisor is
never held accountable for the supervisee's ultimate failure
on the job, should he in fact fail in it, the supervisor should
feel the personal accountability that results from ethical
responsibility if the supervisee's failure may be attributed
in any way to his negligence in providing assistance or

opportunities that might have helped the supervisee to succeed.

Although it is true that social work supervision is by definition a helping process concerned with

> teaching certain contents of knowledge and skill and helping
> workers to learn, . . . [it may be used to] facilitate or obstruct
> the learning process, depending on its nature. . . . The supervisor's gratification in a worker's dependence is sometimes a factor operating against a worker's development.
> This gratification may have led the supervisor to impose
> help, to be authoritative, and to show approval of a worker's
> submissive response [Towle, 1957, pp. 114, 116].

If the supervisor emphasizes getting the job done (both his and the supervisee's), which realistically speaking it is his responsibility to do, but neglects these more subtle and easily overlooked considerations, he is responsive to his responsibility to the agency and perhaps even to its clientele to the extent that they are affected by the supervisee's practice, but he is not responsive to his ethical responsibility to his colleague, the supervisee. The supervisee may indeed perform his assigned agency task better if the supervisor gives him explicit instructions and nurtures his reliance on the supervisor's authoritativeness (more likely his authoritarianism). But the supervisor's ethical responsibility to the supervisee should engender his concern about what happens to the supervisee in the process. Better performance and service may well result from ethical as well as competent supervisory practice, however, because the supervisee may acquire a basis for exercising his independent judgment and hence be able to tackle new situations without waiting for directions from the supervisor.

It is the supervisee's growth on the job that is the supervisor's ethical concern since the supervisory relationship places the supervisor between the supervisee and his

potential for professional growth, no matter who may ultimately benefit from it: the present agency and its clientele
or another agency and its clientele. In other words, the
supervisee's creative development is the supervisor's ethical responsibility, even if such development constitutes
growth beyond the boundaries of agency utility. The dead-
end job, which paraprofessionals and indigenous nonprofessionals are often worried about, need not be a dead
end in the long run if it paves the way for professional
movement elsewhere.

The social worker also owes it to his supervisee to
determine whether there is a correlation between the supervisee's aspirations and opportunities. The supervisee
may have aspirations unsuited to his capacities, opportunities, or preferences. In addition, the social worker owes it
to his supervisee to look ahead to what the supervisee will
face when he leaves the agency, including the resumption
of normal ties to persons with whom he may have had a
different kind of relationship while in the job. (This affects
paraprofessionals and indigenous nonprofessionals particularly.) This obligation exceeds the boundaries of the supervisor's job description but not the boundaries of his
ethical responsibility.

Ethics as well as practicality demands that the supervisee understand what he is expected to do in his job and
the basis on which his performance in it will be appraised.
Whatever the administrative procedures and no matter
how simply they may be satisfied, the supervisor has the
ethical responsibility to let the supervisee know where he
stands in the job and why. Because the supervisor has
power over the supervisee, it is his ethical responsibility to
be certain that written evaluations are accurate, relevant to
the supervisee's job and expectations of him in it, considerate of the circumstances under which the job was done, and
sensitive to the possibility that the information may be misused, misinterpreted, or outdated.

Ethics is thus important in all phases of the supervisory relationship, both before it is formally initiated and after it has ended, insofar as its consequences follow the supervisee. Ethics in supervision need not imply a favorable result for the supervisee, only a just one. The outcome need not be beneficial to the supervisee, only appropriate. Ethics need not result in special advantage for the supervisee, only equity for him. It need not provide the supervisee with preferential opportunities, only safeguards against the genuine hazards he faces because in so many respects he and the supervisor are not equals. The social worker as a supervisor is guided by the Kantian premise that supervisees are not means but ends, and his ethics is a "doctrine of ends," supplying laws for the maxims of action rather than for the actions themselves (Abbott, 1889, pp. 291–292, 299).

When the supervisee is a social work student, placed for supervised practice in an agency by a social work school, a particular order of ethical responsibility is generated. If the student's experience in the agency suggests enough reservations about his general competence to enter the social work profession with a university credential, the supervisor may have to weigh his ethical responsibility to the student against his responsibility to the profession and the community (Levy, 1965a). Despite the supervisor's (or field instructor's) desire to "do good"—that is, to preserve as much as he can of the student and to be fair to him—he may, in effect, have to acknowledge that the boundaries of the usefulness of the student's talents are so narrow that the student cannot be accorded the social work school's professional sanction as a social worker who is sufficiently competent to graduate with the degree in social work. For the graduate of the school of social work, the university degree signifies "beginning competence." This precludes graduating students whose limitations are extensive enough to cast doubt about their readiness to enter the social work profession. The supervisor, for one—since other participants in social work education share responsibility with him—cannot certify such students as eligible for graduation. He carries responsibility not only in relation to the student but in relation to the agency, the school, the profession, and prospective clienteles. He must decide whether his supervisee, from the viewpoint of his work in the agency, should be granted the

> stamp of approval, in the form of a degree, as evidence that he will serve the public competently, honorably, and in accordance with the standards and ethics of the profession. . . . [The supervisor's] moral responsibility in this matter is clear. To graduate incapable and untrustworthy men and women would betray the public trust and render the profession and the public a great disservice [Blauch, 1955, p. 9].

To circle back to the starting point of a social work student's professional career, a risk that candidates for social work education are subjected to consists of negative appraisals of their admissibility to social work school solicited from practitioners with whom they have been in treatment. The ethical issue this poses is whether a social worker should ask for such an appraisal—that is, when the social worker is a faculty member of the school—and whether he should give it when he has been the practitioner. The training analysis is illuminating for the purpose of social work ethics, and has been illuminated in relation to the ethical issue that has been posed. The training analysis is the treatment process that a student psychoanalyst is required to undergo as a requirement for admission to practice. It is thus a therapeutic component of an academic regimen. In effect, one of the "courses" in the student's curriculum is treatment, which is regarded as a requirement for one who will be carrying treatment responsibility. In the training analysis, the candidate is hopefully "changed" so that he masters or disciplines those personal characteristics or modes of behavior that could intrude on his service to others.

Since the training analysis, as its label indicates, is not unrelated to educational objectives, the confidences—articulated and circumstantial—that emerge in it are subject to exposure for evaluative purposes. Educational authorities may resort and have resorted to the training analysis for information and evaluation as a basis for judging candidates' admissibility to practice as psychoanalysts. But Waelder (1962) detected a problem in this:

> The analyst is pledged to secrecy, and this obligation does not merely follow from the condition of privileged communication which is part of the practice of the healing arts; it is also, and specifically, part of the analytic contract in which the patient [i.e., the candidate] has obliged himself to observe, as best he can, the psychoanalytic rule. To convey analytic information to third persons, particularly persons who owe allegiance not to the patient but to an institution, and who have to decide on the satisfaction or frustration of the patient's aspirations introduces a novel element into the analytic situation [p. 285].

Kairys (1964) took a particularly jaundiced view of the training analyst's role in the student's appraisal, both on practice and ethical grounds:

> As we have it today, the training analyst must to some degree report his patient's confidences and be his judge. In the usual training program, the Students' Committee or its equivalent relies heavily on reports from the analyst in making its decisions at each point in the student's progress. Whatever administrative "gimmicks" may be introduced to obscure or minimize the training analyst's role, in the end he inevitably determines when the student starts courses, when he takes his first supervised case, and, above all, when he graduates. In all these decisions, the analyst must step out of his analytic role and intervene crucially in the student's real life [p. 488].

Kairys identified "ecological complications" that muddy the waters for the student and the training analyst alike. The student is exposed to a variety of educational settings. The training analyst is exposed to peers—to their scrutiny and judgment. He develops a "special narcissistic stake" in the student's fate [pp. 493–495]. And contact between the two does not end when the therapeutic analysis terminates. Thus Kairys recommended that the therapeutic function should be completely separated from the evaluative function so that in no way could the latter intrude on the former and so that no confidences, data, or experiences shared in the therapeutic relationship would be used for any purpose but the therapeutic one of the training analysis.

In an interview, Kairys spoke vigorously against the practice by therapists of responding to requests for references for the purpose of appraising a candidate's admissibility to a graduate, psychoanalytic, or any other course of study. He regarded the therapist's transmittal of an appraisal based on a therapeutic relationship as normally reprehensible as well as inappropriate to and intrusive on the therapist's past, present, and future therapeutic function. Such an act, in Kairys' judgment, constituted an unwarranted betrayal of a confidence. The fact that the therapist might also be involved or interested in the educational program to which the patient or client was applying was only an additional though not unimportant complication.

Kairys had considerable doubt about the pertinence of therapeutic data and revelations for reference purposes: for example, in connection with admittance to college or graduate professional education. "What relevance," he asked in the interview, "would data about symptoms or pathology have to an applicant's potential as a student, a social worker, a psychiatrist, and so on?" He doubted both the validity and utility of a therapist's participation in any of these forms of appraisal. He insisted that it was a kind of malum in se and absolutely unnecessary. There were other, more relevant methods of obtaining an evaluation. His underlying premise, however, was that the therapist owed a prior responsibility to the patient or client and not to his colleagues. If responsibility is owed to others for providing controls to insure that only persons with adequate capacity to learn and to become ethical and competent practitioners will be admitted to sensitive fields of practice, Kairys said, the therapist is not the appropriate medium for implementing that responsibility. And, he added,

> present practices are hardly airtight anyhow. Incompetents and unsuitable persons do squeeze through. The risks run by seeking out private data, not necessarily related to practice competence and aptitude, are not warranted by the unconfirmed presumption that the interests of society are thus protected—which they may not be anyway. It is better to rely on normal educational processes rather than run these risks [compare Kairys, pp. 508–510].

The training analysis—admittedly complex—and commentaries on it have been explored at length because of their pertinence for social work and because of the applicability to social work of the ethical judgments cited. Apropos of the social worker's relationship with colleagues and prospective colleagues, one might go even further and suggest that he has the ethical responsibility not to reveal or *use* in such connections any private information about them (whether or not obtained in confidence or in a therapeutic relationship).

Before this discussion ends, and it hardly exhausts either the issues or the ethical principles that are applicable to the social worker's relationship to the various categories of colleagues, the following question should be asked about the ethics of informing: Should a social worker who is aware of a colleague's unethical conduct, particularly in relation to a client, deal with it in some direct way or, if he cannot, should he report it to whatever medium exists for dealing with it and work toward some kind of constructive influence, censure, restraint, control, or discipline? The answer, despite the strictures of professional etiquette is yes. The social worker is expected to be ethical and to see to it that his colleagues are ethical, too. This is a risky principle for it makes possible the harassment and abuse of colleagues, but it is an ethical responsibility, and it must be responsibly and thoughtfully implemented. It is a way of saying that ethics begins at home.

Chapter 16

SOCIAL WORKERS AND UNIONS

The reconciliation of conflicting ethical responsibilities toward the various persons and organizations to whom the social worker has been said to owe ethical responsibility becomes especially problematic when the question of the social worker's participation in unions is raised. On the face of it, the social worker's very affiliation with a union, let alone his engaging in work stoppages of any kind during labor-management conflicts, seems to violate his commitment to give "precedence" to his "professional responsibility" over his personal interests ("Profession of Social Work").

The appropriateness of union affiliation and participation for social workers (as well as for members of other professions and particularly the human service professions), although more generally confirmed in recent years than in the past, is not yet universally unquestioned.[1] A reason for this is the concern about the social worker's professional status and about the prospect that the social worker will have to engage in certain aggressive activities in implementing union goals. In addition, many social workers are hard put to align themselves with a medium of representation and action that has traditionally been associated with labor and the "working class." One problem often faced in unions that social workers do affiliate themselves with is whether to join forces with nonprofessional employees and, if so, whether to negotiate collectively with them. Not infrequently, the interests of each group are negotiated separately, although both groups participate and lend each other moral and even practical support.

Finally (and this is a veritable clinker), because social workers, in their professional capacity, are often found in the camps of both labor and management, they find themselves, on the one hand, committed to the same professional ethics, and, on the other, representing conflicting interests.

There are specific hazards connected with unionization, and no rationalization can easily dismiss them. For example, even when union affiliation is regarded as proper for social workers, certain union actions, such as the strike, appear to militate against maximum fidelity and service to clients. Confidentiality may be endangered, or clients in need may be neglected. A strike, picketing, or a sudden work-stoppage does seem to contravene the ethical obligation not to withdraw from a service relationship without "good cause," which usually means at the client's instance or provocation. As it was expressed by a group of lawyers

[1]For example, Strauss (1964) regarded the union issue as a dilemma for engineers so it must be at least that to social workers and members of other human service professions for whom the same issue still recurs.

in relation to the ethics of lawyers and is undoubtedly applicable to social workers:

> A lawyer is a fiduciary. If he joins the union he cannot escape being subjected to a struggle between loyalties pulling him in opposite directions. The question is not whether he may resist the temptation to act adversely to his client, but whether he should voluntarily subject himself to such temptation. It is the tug on his conscience that is significant and should be avoided [Opinion No. 376, 1956, p. 766.]

More permissive views have been expressed by lawyers and others since this opinion was published. Lawyers of the Legal Aid Society actually went out on strike during an impasse in their negotiations with the society with no particular doubt about their right to do so—on professional grounds certainly—although varied perspectives were entertained about the issues being negotiated. Permissive points of view were expressed quite early in relation to social workers, despite the great tension generated by charges of communistic control over social work unions during the disruptive era of Senator Joseph McCarthy (e.g., Fitch, 1950).

The current view generally is that no ethical issue is posed by union affiliation and participation, whether in a union of the "trade" variety (social workers only) or the industrial variety (professional and nonprofessional workers). What remains a concern, however, is the comportment of social workers in a union capacity or activity that can be interpreted as conflicting with the social worker's ethical responsibility to clients and others. The right to strike is usually upheld—not without considerable strain for unionized social workers as well as others—as long as it is not at the expense of clients for whom provision can be and usually is made.

The right to participate in unions, and to strike if necessary, is based on the premise that, professional or not, social workers who work for agencies, institutions, or organizations are employees, i.e., workers. As employees they need opportunities to represent their own interests. Particularly in times of high unemployment, social workers may feel vulnerable in the face of their employers' relative power, or at least feel the need to have their interests effectively represented and safeguarded. In this respect, social workers are in the position of employees everywhere and at every level of responsibility. That is, unless they bargain and act collectively, they are liable to be given short shrift.

The plight of employees generally is only relatively better than it was in the nineteenth and the first half of the twentieth century. For some employee groups, conditions are scarcely better at all, although some laws do protect them in some ways. Since social agencies are not profit-making enterprises, and the pressure of monetary rewards and the interests of stockholders do not operate, the vulnerability of their employees tends to increase. Representatives of their managements are not apt to panic if staff members threaten to strike, except to the extent that they identify with the clienteles, service to whom may be affected. The influence of such identification rarely matches the influence of fiscal considerations. In short, despite occasional shifts in the locus of power, employees as a group—social workers included—tend to be disadvantaged in comparison with employers. There has been considerable improvement in the lot of the working man or woman in the past half-century. Legal, social, and other restraints, on the one hand, and the emergence of the labor movement, on the other, have done much to protect employees from cavalier abuse or neglect by employers. However, this is true only to a limited extent, especially when economic conditions are bad.

It is not only the power to hire and fire that makes the difference in the work life and status of an employee, union contracts to the contrary notwithstanding. Authority over employees at any level may count as much and often more. An employee may be as intimidated by the person who determines the kind or quantity of work he will be required to do or appraises the quality of the work he has done, as he is by the person who is authorized to lay him off. An employee may be more directly affected by one who has immediate jurisdiction over the specific conditions of his work than by one who can decide whether he will work at all.

Despite social legislation and other regulatory mechanisms, employees do not enjoy a symmetrical relationship with employers—including those employers who happen to be social workers, as administrators of social agencies often are. Not only are their functions different, and hence asymmetrical or nonreciprocal, but their relative capacities to effect control over, or influence on each other are also different.

In some respects, unions have been placed under greater statutory restraint in the United States than they were a generation or two ago. Nevertheless, there is little evidence that public policy holds labor to be an adversary that is equal in power to management. Much has been done by way of legislation and public administration to reduce what could be regarded as a union's unfair advantage over management or as union leadership's advantage over its own membership, but little has been done to suggest that, as of this moment, labor is the equal of management in power or opportunity. This has been no less true during periods of prosperity and "full" employment than during periods of recession. It was absolutely untrue during the Great Depression and the years preceding it, both the fat years and the lean years. It is not true today.

Judicial recognition has been accorded this fact. Chief Justice Hughes (*National Labor Relations Board* v. *Jones and Laughlin Steel Corporation,* 1937) held that the National Labor Relations Act of 1935 safeguarded the fundamental right of employees to organize themselves, and to select their own representatives for the purpose of collective bargaining and mutual protection, without being subject to their employer's restraint or coercion.

And in the case of *American Steel Foundries* v. *Tri-City Central Trades Council* (1921) to which Justice Hughes referred, Chief Justice Taft enunciated reasons for equalizing the chances of employees in their confrontations with employers.

> Is interference of a labor organization by persuasion and appeal to induce a strike against low wages, under such circumstances, without lawful excuse and malicious? We think not. Labor unions are recognized by the Clayton [i.e., Federal Anti-Trust] Act as legal when instituted for mutual help and lawfully carrying out their legitimate objects. They have long been thus recognized by the courts. They were organized out of the necessities of the situation. A single employee was helpless in dealing with an employer. He was dependent ordinarily on his daily wage for the maintenance of himself and his family. If the employer refused to pay him the wages that he thought fair, he was nevertheless unable to leave the employ and to resist arbitrary and unfair treatment. Union was essential to give laborers opportunity to deal on an equality with their employer [p. 199].

Similar judgments have been made about social work unions. The chief issue to be contended with here, however, is the ethics of the social worker in relation to unions, whether he is a union member or an employer. When, as union members or employers, social workers deal or negotiate with each other, "the plain fact is . . . that . . . conflict is inevitable [Willauer, 1951, p. 140]."[2]

Where unions of professional social workers are concerned, conflicts are not only inevitable between labor and management; they are inevitable within the ranks of union

---

[2]This part of the discussion draws freely on Levy (1964).

members and within the ranks of administrative representatives, whether they are executives (i.e., professional personnel) or volunteers (i.e., lay personnel). These conflicts
stem from the inherent nature of labor management relations and from the specific expectations of personnel engaged in social work enterprises.

There is little doubt that some of the conflict that
social workers experience in unions derives from their
sense of responsibility both to their clients and to their
agency. And some of the conflict experienced by management representatives in social agencies derives from their
conception of their responsibility to staff members, which
is influenced by the social work philosophy that shapes the
character of the services that social agencies provide.

True enough, this conflict is a residue of modern social
work practice; there was less embarrassment in the management group about the social deprivation of the labor
group until the late nineteenth and early twentieth century.
If Jane Addams was not the minion of the labor group, she
was hardly the darling of the industrial management group.
She was much too helpful to the union movement to merit
the kudos of management. From her point of view, moreover, she was far too sensitive about employers' oppression
of unsuspecting immigrants to be kindly disposed toward
them. In fact, she complained about the "tainted money"
contributed to Hull House by a donor "who was notorious
for underpaying the girls in his establishment" and was
hardly inclined to accept his munificence unquestioningly.
Nevertheless, in her zeal for justice, Miss Addams and Hull
House were subjected to as much scrutiny by labor as by
capital (Addams, 1961, 106–107, Chap. 10).

For a time, social agencies were viewed as the pawns
of capital, and not always without justification.

> Workers saw powerful social agencies openly aligned
> against the burgeoning trade unions. They saw employing
> groups occasionally utilize these agencies as frank instru-

ments for breaking strikes. They saw some of these agencies deliberately withold relief from the families of striking workers, pressuring able-bodied men and women on relief rolls to serve as scabs in struck factories. And they saw opportunistic directors of social agencies bid openly for contributions from the rich on the ground that private social work kept the lower classes satisfied, that it helped suppress strikes and even revolutionary tendencies among the ignorant, "debased" masses of society [Deutsch, 1944, pp. 290–291].

The charitable services did not always seem so charitable and were sometimes regarded as incompatible with the proletarian ideology of an unrestricted union movement. As one observer viewed it:

The leaders of the trade unions, who regarded the manufacturers *a priori* as a class enemy, resented the charities sending clients to work in struck plants, operating non-union shops, furnishing cheap labor and undermining union wage schedules [Silver, 1962, p. 10].

Add to history the intimidation of a code of ethics that stresses responsibility for continued service to agency clients (Rehr, 1960) and the conflict about work stoppages and other union devices becomes oppressive to conscientious social workers. On the other hand, emphasize the civil rights implications of personnel practices codes and the Bill of Rights, and management representatives suffer agonies of conscience when resisting the representations of union representatives, though mindful of their accountability for contributors' funds. Executives who are social workers, however, are slung midway between the interests of both because, as professional colleagues of union representatives, they are impelled to be considerate of the personnel's welfare, but as representatives of management they are obliged to be considerate of the agency's resources.

Despite the pulls in opposite directions on the participants in labor-management relations, labor-management conflict may truly be viewed as a "socially constructive force [Willauer, 1951, p. 140]." Unfortunately, however, representatives of unions and management who are social workers, tend to confuse their roles in the process of negotiation, which militates against the effective performance of the social function of labor-management relations (Goldberg, 1960).

For effective and ethical labor-management relations, representatives of labor are obliged to represent labor, and representatives of management are obliged to represent management. There is little room for the kind of objectivity and empathy that are required for social work service. Professional discipline is inappropriate. On the other hand, some of the principles of interpersonal relations that are characteristic of social work practice and administration may help to accomplish the ends of labor-management relations without unduly violating some of the more sacred principles of social work practice.

This does not mean, however, that social workers, because they are bound by a professional code of behavior, are deprived of the right or opportunity to take active and organized steps to ensure their own material welfare. Such steps do not necessarily contravene the assumption of primary responsibility to agency clients, although certain stipulations to safeguard the welfare of agency clients are assumed. Therefore, the statement that Virginia P. Robinson made with such conviction in 1937 may be considered archaic, although it might have been deemed quite pertinent at the time:

> If you can accept with me that service to the client is the essential purpose for which these [welfare] agencies exist, their "product" if you will, and that we would like to see that product as good as possible; if you can accept with me further that the quality of this service grows out of the functioning of the agency as a whole, of the participation of every

worker in this service, you may understand something of the
problem the union creates when it treats a social work
agency as an industrial organization and cuts the administrative and supervisory functions off from other functions in an
effort to make them like managing functions in industry.
This they are not and cannot be made to be [1937].

The more modern, although hardly unanimous view, which
is as applicable to social agencies as it is to industry is that

> labor management conflict . . . is the interaction of aggres-
> sive labor and management groups within the moderating
> influence of the American social structure that is producing
> revised definitions of the rights and obligations of the indi-
> vidual.
>   The basic right through which the concept of civil lib-
> erty must find expression and application in our industrial
> system is the right of workers to bargain collectively with
> their employers. It is in the exercise of this right that the
> individual gains a voice in the determination of the condi-
> tions under which he works and under which he and his
> family live [Willauer, 1951, pp. 140–141].

Social workers and their families are as subject to adverse conditions of employment as are personnel in industry, and consequently they are as entitled to represent their
interests through union negotiation as are employees in
any industry. Similarly, administrative representatives of
social agencies are as accountable for the expenditure of
agency funds as are management personnel in industry and
consequently are as obliged to represent the interests of
contributors and agency beneficiaries as management personnel are to represent owners and stockholders. Hopefully, however, both union and management
representatives will be guided by their concern for agency
clients and by agency philosophy and thus accord to one
another maximum consideration and strive to resolve
differences amicably and considerately so that services will

be sustained at a maximum level without undue penalty either to staff or to agency.

Inevitably, the issue of the strike emerges for, as Arthur J. Goldberg (1951) put it when he served as a legal counselor to unions,

> the right to bargain collectively necessarily implies the right to strike. The possibility of a strike if negotiations fail is the premise and the incentive which alone can lead to successful collective bargaining. Otherwise there can be no content to the bargaining because there is no terminal point which the parties must both attempt to avoid [p. 150].

That the representatives of both labor and management are duty bound to avoid a strike if they possibly can is implicit in this view of labor-management relations and particularly labor-management relations in social agencies. What is at stake is not merely the profit of an enterprise or the productivity of personnel in that enterprise but the welfare of clientele who do not have the kind of power possessed by purchasing consumers of a marketable product to enforce a reconciliation, and who are instead perhaps dependent on the availability of the agency's service.

> In such activities . . . it is reasonable to say that strikes should never occur. But . . . do we mean that the responsibility for the avoidance of strikes rests upon the workers alone? Or is there an indefinable body known as the public, as well? If we think that the sole responsibility is that of the worker, we are, in effect, saying that when a person chooses a career involving particularly exacting and essential service, he has by that choice lost his right to protest . . . obligations run both ways. If strikes are "unthinkable," so is disregard of the workers' welfare and point of view [Fitch, 1950, pp. 10–11].

Strikes would probably not become necessary if the representatives of both labor and management committed themselves to resolving their differences, even to the extent of

submitting their otherwise insoluble differences to mutually acceptable impartial third-party referees.

Given the background of the discussion in the last few
chapters, the ethics of social work participants in labor-
management relations is hardly obscure, whether those
participants represent employees or management.[3] They
must ever be guided by the ethics of their profession, both
in the pursuit of their professional responsibility and in
their personal conduct as social workers.

As agency employees social workers have the right to
participate actively in organized efforts designed to improve their employment conditions. This assumption is
based, on the one hand, on the recognition of their legal
and moral rights as citizens in a democracy and, on the
other, on the recognition of the importance of employment
conditions that provide for their own and their families'
economic and other requirements sufficiently to make possible their maximum attention to their professional responsibility.

As practitioners with responsibility for service to members of the community and with an abiding concern for
their health and welfare, social workers set a high priority
on maintaining and improving social services to the community. They are prepared to devote their energy and their
professional skill to implementing these services, and prepared to do all within their power and resources to prevent
any interruption or impairment of these services. At the
same time, they owe to themselves and their families the
responsibility to act in their own behalf as agency employees.

As members of a professional association, they have

___

[3]The following propositions are derived from a preamble to a policy
statement on labor-management relations adopted by the Metropolitan
Association of Jewish Center Workers of New York in 1961, which the
author prepared in his capacity as chairman of the committee that had
been appointed to formulate such a statement.

the opportunity to define and act on standards of behavior and practice that will ensure the maintenance and improvement of agency services. As members of unions, they also have the opportunity to participate in processes that will ensure for them democratic and effective means of representing their interests as employees and as members of their profession.

Since the professional association includes practitioners at both management and employee levels of agency participation, principles to guide professional workers in their role in labor-management relations validly relate to both levels of participation. This consideration carries with it the implication that professional agency personnel at all levels of participation share concern about the following: the nature and continuity of agency service to agency clientele, responsibility for conduct that is consistent with the professional ethics they are identified with, and a preference for personnel standards that will be duly considerate of the needs of agency personnel as well as agency clientele.

The role that management personnel play in labor-management relations is determined by their responsibility as agency executives, and the role of employees who belong to the bargaining unit is determined by the unit's goals and procedures. Hopefully, labor and management representatives—both in the agency board and on the staff —as well as other parties in interest, will proceed at all times with a commitment to exhaust every and all legitimate and valid democratic instrumentalities of labor-management negotiations to resolve differences constructively and equitably, in relation to the interests of both groups, so that agency services may continue uninterrupted and so that the dignity of all participants can be properly safeguarded.

The responsibility to avoid work-stoppages or intrusions upon the atmosphere of service to clients is shared by social workers in both union and management positions. Both share responsibility for provisions for maintaining necessary services to clients in the event that service is interrupted, whether through strikes, lockouts, stoppages, slowdowns, or picketing. Both are enjoined from exploiting clients when implementing their labor-management goals.

Similarly, students placed for field instruction in agencies affected by labor-management conflicts must not be exploited for either labor's or management's purposes. Social work students are placed in agencies to obtain professional education. A work stoppage interferes, atmospherically if not actually, with this purpose. Students should therefore not be expected to cross a picketline or participate in it. They should not be required to commit themselves either in favor of, or against a union or management action, regardless of where their personal sympathies lie. As students, they are neither employees nor union members, and should therefore not be expected to participate as if they are, nor be used because they are not.

The labor-management relations of social workers in staff and managerial positions are fraught with ethical hazards, which is all the more reason for maximum clarity about the roles they play and the ethics by which they must be guided in playing them.

Chapter 17

USES OF A SOCIAL WORK CODE OF ETHICS

I have sometimes been asked why a profession should have
a code of ethics which its members are required to observe
over and above any requirements laid on them by law and
commercial usage. . . .

Members of professions enjoy a standing in the community which comes from a sense of service, if need be at times
with little or no reward, from the maintenance of a standard
of competence in professional work, as well as from a standard of behavior in public and private life. . . . We are as
human as anybody else, and a code of conduct is a help and
not a hindrance provided that it is reasonable and applied
with understanding and forbearance. . . .

The Fundamental Rules [of the code] . . . are by no
means easy to apply in contemporary conditions [Croxton-
Smith, 1965a, p. 749].

Codes of ethics are at once the highest and the lowest
standards of conduct expected of practitioners; the awesome statement of rigid requirements and the pro forma
blurb issued primarily for public relations purposes; the

gradually evolved essence of moral expectations and the arbitrarily concocted shortcut to professional prestige and status; the handy guide for the legal enforcement of ethical conduct and for punishment for the infringements thereof, or the unrealistic, unimpressive, and generally unknown or ignored guide to wishful thinking.

Codes of ethics come in all forms and all sizes. They may consist of brief creeds, long credos, or numerous canons. They may be as spiritual as the message from Sinai or as earthy and sparse as the limits of liability on the back of a parking stub. They may be as lofty as the virtues enunciated by Plato and Aristotle or as picayune as the proprieties propounded by Emily Post.

Codes of ethics are many different things to many different persons, whether or not in the occupations for which they are designed. They are many things, though not always effective. If they did not exist in most of the occupations in which they do exist, they would undoubtedly have to be invented.

The need they serve is not always measurable, any more than is the effectiveness with which they meet any concrete need, but they do serve a function in society, variable as it may be for various occupations and for the times and circumstances in which they operate. In some occupations they serve a rather special function (McGee, 1963):

> Any social group, if it is to survive as a group, will develop complexes of conduct which become fixed in the behavior of that group. When these patterns of conduct become sufficiently conscious to be cited by those who would censure and direct—and those who would do so will include in some degree all in the community—we can speak of the mores of that society; to speak of a society without mores is to speak of a virtual impossibility. . . . For most of those in the group its customs—felt perhaps with all the force of law—require no justification. They exist: some things are done, and some things are not done. . . . Prescriptive customs, mores, are

> prior in time to explicit and explicitly defined ethical rules
> . . . the development of community life may make feasible
> and desirable the formulation and peculiarly detached de-
> velopment of ethical rules: rules which through their norma-
> tive formulation are freed from dependence on the facts of
> social life: rules which are distinguishable from descriptions
> or expressions of custom: rules which can be clearly re-
> garded *as* rules. Such rules and systems of rules represent
> an articulation and transformation of implicit patterns of
> moral judgment and conduct. . . .
>
> An ethical statement is no longer a report or expression
> of mores: it is custom transformed into rule, an explicit
> formalization of the prescriptive customs of the group, de-
> liberately advanced and wielded as a regulative principle
> [pp. 201–202].

The customs and standards of an occupation are dou-
ble-edged swords, whether or not they are intended to be.
They may be explicitly enforceable through elaborate ma-
chinery, which occasionally does exist and does constitute
part and parcel of codified customs and standards. They
can also represent a considerable influence on the conduct
of practitioners. What practitioners perceive as the behavioral expectations of peers, because they are codified customs and standards in their occupation, often carry the
force of law and sometimes even greater force. An infringe-
ment of such customs and standards requires only that the
offending practitioner himself be aware of it and be concerned about it, on pain of pangs of personal conscience or
dread of his peers' disapproval.

Hegel (*Encyclopedia of Philosophy*) evidently took something like this into account when he made the following
observation:

> The developed totality of business and labor organizes itself
> in complete professional groups. Each represents profes-
> sional ethical codes and each is represented by individual
> agents in which alone those codes are actual. Such concrete
> laws are effective, as a second nature composed of habits and
> accepted customs or standards of the groups.

The universal exchange of socially organized practical functions is the work of the whole, in which the individual shares the profits and towards which he contributes his share and care. "Individual satisfactions are mediated through the work of all."

Ethical culture (*Bildung*) exists in the individual so far as he makes himself fit to take place in a social professional pattern; and to achieve his recognition as cooperating with others in common concerns. This is integrity (*Ehre*) and rightness (*Rechtschaffenheit*).

While division of labor, on one hand, is the precondition for such social value or virtue of the individual; on the other hand, it leads to greater and greater socialization of functions, dependent more and more on impersonal connections. Skills thus become more and more mechanical and replaceable like machines [pp. 248–249].

Although it is true that occupational groups are sometimes motivated by a zeal for respectability, to conceive of, or concoct a codification of principles or standards of conduct, more often than not they are moved by a genuine need for guides to action in situations of agonizing conflict and by the sincere aspiration to deal justly with clients, colleagues, and society. The ethical issues practitioners face are often extremely troublesome and, although they suffer no delusion that a neat compilation of precepts will solve all their ethical problems or eliminate all unethical conduct, they do crave some kinds of criteria or consensus that might, at times, at least serve as a basis for action choices.

The need for a code of ethics as a consensual guide, at least for use by practitioners, is a rather old one, and it has persisted despite varying degrees of attention and despite results of varying degrees of definitiveness. The Pagan Oath of Hippocrates (Jones, 1955) comes readily even to a school child's mind as an early formulation of a code of ethics that endures sturdily, although revision and updating have been earnestly proposed (Lasagna, 1964). It certainly stresses the physician's ethical responsibility to patients in particular and to the medical profession and society in general, and provides some extraordinarily specific cues for his ethical conduct. And, ever since, other occupational groups have, with greater or lesser definitiveness, formulated codes of their own. The quest for a code has hardly been the exclusive concern of the human service or helping professions, but it has clearly been a special preoccupation among them. As Hailman (1949) observed:

> Each profession was established with the basic purpose of service to humanity. This is the distinguishing feature of a profession. Each felt that in order to render this human service the profession would have to be united around basic ethical principles and in a professional self-regulatory organization. As a means of carrying out this service in an ethical manner, each profession has put great stress on continuous professional education and on help to be given by older members of the group to younger or newer members. Some professions have used regulation by law, but this regulation has never been the chief factor in maintaining ethical standards. All these means are used to achieve a high level of performance, without encroaching on the essential democratic rights of each individual in the profession [p. 44].

Hailman described the social worker's need—"in concrete terms"—for a code at a time when social workers had no code and were engaged in an arduous effort to consider and formulate one:

> Primarily, social workers want and need definite, recognized standards of professional conduct to guide them in their dealings with clients, fellow workers, employers, the community, and the general public.
> Social workers, like other professional workers, are daily faced with the necessity for making a choice between conflicting lines of conduct. A code should help resolve these conflicts, although obviously it will not be the answer to all problems [p. 45].

The shaping of a code of ethics, and even its scrupulous enforcement within or outside of statutory and judicial instrumentalities, is scarcely the key to occupational purification, either in human service professions or in profit-making business enterprises. On the contrary, codes of ethics are by no means the most compelling influence on the ethical conduct of practitioners. Still, they serve for many practitioners, in varying degrees and in a variety of ways, at least an integrative function of some kind[1] and perhaps even serve as a rather necessary aid to what practitioners may sincerely regard as necessary conformity, notwithstanding their zealous regard for independence and freedom to practice.[2]

Monypenny (1955) has summarized rather felicitously some of the broad values and uses of codes of ethics that further explain the industrious pursuit of codes by so many occupations (Hailman estimated as early as 1949 that "over two hundred business and professional groups in the United States have adopted codes of ethics since 1890," p. 44):

> The action of various professional groups in adopting ethical codes suggests that there is some value in a formal state-

[1]Compare Hartmann's (1960) discussion of Freud's view of "ethics in the strictest sense, in contrast to the psychological study of moral behavior." It "was not a field very close to Freud's heart [p. 14]."

[2]"Obviously, there are many *kinds* of conformity. If some are bad, some should be preserved at all costs. Some non-conformities are license rather than purposeful and creative. 'The effect of liberty to individuals is that they may do as they please,' said Edmund Burke. ... It seems to me that conformity is good when it involves those conventional forms, those niceties of conduct which are the customary cues to our respect for one another. They are the signs of reciprocity of consideration in human affairs. ... 'Must we conform?' Of course. And in the process far from ceasing to be men, we fulfill ourselves [Wilson, 1964, p. 31]." Codes of ethics may quite accurately be regarded as the codified conventions of occupations.

ment of obligations which goes beyond those defined in the law. What such a code rests on is the identification of the individual with the group, an identification which includes his acceptance of group standards and his susceptibility to group action, whether of disapproval or approbation. Every working group determines to some extent the professional future of its members as the group evaluates their conduct and reacts to that conduct. . . . The future of the individual and his immediate satisfaction in his work depend in part on judgments within the group [p. 101].

Professional practitioners rarely believe that a code of ethics can ever be an inherently effective and useful mechanism of control to insure ethical conduct on the part of their peers; nor do they usually entertain the hope or expectation that the code of ethics will have the effect of *enforcing* ethical conduct, even by indirection. Rather, practitioners who have given particular thought to the matter, prefer to regard the code of ethics as an enabling rather than an intimidating medium of influence, and toward that end they exert every possible effort at all levels of occupational association to *implement* the code of ethics rather than *enforce* it.

The distinction between the two objectives that might be envisaged for a code of ethics—that is, enforcement and implementation—has been revealingly articulated in the following manner by the National Education Association (1964):

There has been confusion between the concepts of enforcement and of implementation of the Code of Ethics of the Education Profession. Although various individuals in the profession have talked and written for years about the need to enforce the Code, many in the profession have been reluctant to do so. Enforcement has implied an approach which places foremost attention on the use of the "big stick" or the means of last resort, because the term "enforcement" means formal action leading to censure, suspension or expulsion from the organization. Implementation, by contrast,

is interpreted to mean that primary emphasis is placed upon
raising professional standards by providing effective guidance and counseling. In the event that other means fail to
provide an equitable solution, professional association enforcement procedures must be available as part of the total
implementation program, but this is subsidiary to raising
professional standards [p. 1].

The essayed distinction between enforcement and implementation makes quite evident the reliance of some occupations (evidence suggests that this affects *most*
occupations) on group *influence* rather than group *pressure.*

The codes of ethics of a few occupations (in some
jurisdictions as few as one, the legal profession) do have the
force of law, which reduces occupational opportunity for
leisurely influence, although it does not eliminate this opportunity. The use of influence is still very much in evidence in the legal profession and in other occupations in
which occupational and legal sanctions are highly integrated. At any rate, codes of ethics do exist and do constitute some kind of normative influence for individuals or
occupations or both, and occasionally also for legislatures
or tribunals.

Even an inclusive and clear code of ethics does not
suffice to induce idealized standards of professional conduct, in practice and out. On the contrary, a code of ethics
can only serve as a general guide and as a record of professional consensus. By and large, behavioral choices remain
the province of each practitioner, who inevitably faces circumstances that do not lend themselves to precise choices
and to precise applications of the codified guides. Often
there are also conflicts of choice based on the various categories of ethical responsibility. Rarely is the ultimate decision self-evident.

Still, the broader the range of considerations for which
the code of ethics provides, the greater the possibility of

awareness on the practitioner's part concerning the bases for his action choices, which he is required to take into account. Similarly, the codification and clarification of the ethical principles to which the profession subscribes serve as an explicit guide for professional education and supervision, which can be used to assist students and social workers in developing their understanding of the principles and their skill in applying them in practice and experience.

A deficiency affecting the code of ethics of the National Association of Social Workers, aside from its lack of inclusiveness, is the lack of an unambiguous system of implementation and enforcement. True, grievance and review procedures do exist, but more desirable is a consistent and autonomous mechanism that can continue to expand, clarify, and interpret the meaning of the code; mediate issues and complaints which may emerge in relation to it; and adjudicate alleged offenses.

The quest for clarification and interpretation does not need to await conflicts. It can be a continuous process, as it is in the law, for example. Cases may be hypothesized for the purpose of clarity about the meaning of the code, or be adjudicated when they actually arise, to serve on the one hand as precedents for future cases and to insure justice and good practice and, on the other, to serve as an improved guide for practitioners. (Attempts have been made in this direction; see, for example, National Association of Social Workers, Commission on Social Work Ethics.)

Though hardly inept, the code of ethics of the National Association of Social Workers[1] must be regarded as still embryonic in form. This is not a mean achievement for a

[1]The National Federation of Societies for Clinical Social Work has compiled its own code of ethics which differs from the NASW code in some interesting ways, notably in its explication of principles of ethical social work practice and in its expressed concern for the effect of the social worker's practice on the client's welfare (1974).

relatively young profession. However, there is much by way of experience and documentation available to help hasten the development of social work's code as well as its ethics.

Chapter 18

IMPLEMENTING SOCIAL WORK ETHICS

An editorial ("The Code of Ethics and Its Implementation") in the professional journal of the Canadian Association of Social Workers noted with alarm the incidence in the press of items pertaining to the professional conduct of members of "other professions" that required disciplinary action by ethics and disciplinary committees of various professional groups. The editorial then went on to express puzzlement concerning the social work profession:

> To our knowledge, such formal action [for violations of the code of ethics] has never been taken by our association.
>
> Is this not in some ways most surprising? How can we explain it? Does it mean the professional conduct of our members has always been of an exemplary nature: that we have been unclear of our position; or that the procedures by which we enforce our code of ethics have been ineffectual or nonexistent?
>
> Unfortunately, regardless of the strength and dedication motivating our practice, we can never completely rise

> above human frailty, and thus the possibility of improper,
> unacceptable behavior is ever present. This possibility ne-
> cessitates workable machinery and clear-cut processes for
> dealing with infractions [p. 76].

The editorial also complained that the association's code of ethics "lacks specificity and clarity" and declared that "the time has come to state our positions on desirable profes-sional conduct and to spell out the consequences of failure to meet these levels."

This statement expresses the need, within the social work profession as well as outside it, for some form of regulation and enforcement of social work ethics. It is an acknowledgement of the "grave responsibilities" of social workers "related to the lives and well-being of their clients [Boudreau, 1965, p. 11]."

Boudreau summarized as non-legal, those methods of professional regulation that are not backed by the police power of the community and are typically under the control of the professional association; and as legal, those through which formal authority or sanction is delegated either to the professional association or some other vehicle to en-force professional standards and ethics.

> Those who advocate legal regulation of social work feel that
> it is the only way to achieve control over the profession, as
> they feel that the present methods of regulation [when legal
> regulation has not been legislated] are ineffective and that
> non-legal methods do not carry the necessary force [p. 14].[1]

When social workers are employed by social agencies, a degree of control is expected within the structure of the

[1]For cumulative accounts of regulatory legislation enacted in various jurisdictions see, for example, *NASW News* (October-November, 1972, February, 1973). See also, the resolution on the "Regulation of Social Work Practice," adopted by the NASW Delegate Assembly in 1964.

agency, which has some jurisdiction over its staff and assumes some responsibility for its conduct (Boudreau, 1965, pp. 12–13). However, not all of the acts of social workers are amenable to observation and scrutiny, even in agencies, so that this is not altogether a reliable basis of control. Social workers usually meet clients in relative privacy. As far as groups and committees are concerned, deviations are not always detectable.

Legal regulation, is more inclusive than is germane to the focus of this discussion because it usually includes qualifications and the right to practice social work in general, which are implicit in provisions for certification, registration, and licensing. (For the functional distinctions among these media of regulation, see Turner, 1954, p. 69.)

However, it is not only parsimony that influences this limitation on the present discussion. For one thing, although the law is commonly viewed as incorporating and formalizing ethics, not all law is ethical and not all ethics finds itself legislated into law. Much law, in fact, is unethical, if not in its provisions, then in its operation. Representative Charles Vanik of Ohio, for example, recently observed that large profit-making corporations, in not paying their just share of taxes or any at all, were "not doing anything illegal," although there might be something unjust about their failure to do so (New York Post, December 19, 1974).

Cohen (1961), expressed a similar view in more general terms:

> In discussing the relation of law to justice it is well to distinguish between the formal and the material, between justice before the law and justice in the law. The classical maxim, "justice is giving everyone his due," is applicable to legal procedure, where it means that the judge or administering officials should be impartial, i.e., honestly follow the law and not extend favors or disfavors to those who are not legally entitled to them. But the content of laws thus scrupulously obeyed may itself be most unjust [p. 15].

More pertinently, however, when ethics is legislated and becomes law, a violation is by definition a legal offense. An offender breaks the law and is subject to legal penalties as a result. The greater problem as far as social work ethics is concerned is to inspire ethical conduct without regard to law. The aim is a kind of "moral discipline" that

> directs as well as informs us. It guides, and guidance is distinct from influence. We speak of a principle of morality as guiding, not simply influencing action. . . . It is principles . . . that are self-evident, not our absolute duties in concrete moral situations. These principles are apprehended by reason, for our intuitive insights are insights of reason [McCloskey, 1962, pp. 11, 15–16].

L. K. Hall (1952) did not think that it was "possible to reduce conduct in all situations to simple rules," or that "to add rule to rule" produced "a complete code of ethical behavior." Moreover, he doubted that obeying all the rules made "one an ethical person. . . . A truly ethical person does not mind having to keep on thinking things through, turning the general principle into concrete behavior in given situations [p. 5]." Regulation of social work ethics, in other words, is not only a matter of legal or other external controls but of internal control. And

> cultural imperatives can become personal desires . . . Although social roles are prescribed by the cultural heritage, their performance is motivated by the expectation of satisfying personality needs. Though these roles must be performed so that their functions for society can be served, individuals desire to perform because personal functions are thereby served [Spiro, 1961, pp. 105–106].

What must be generated is the kind of "cognitive dissonance" that John Platt (1970) considered to be a

> precondition for any kind of personal learning—that is, reorganization—experience. . . . Strong cognitive dissonance,

personal or social, has many side effects (system instabili-
ties) such as anxiety, anger, over-assertion (pro- or anti-
status quo) or counter-responses such as withdrawal, nausea
and melancholy, which accounts for the sense of relief when
it is resolved [p. 4].

Such psychological or biological upheaval may not be necessary, but what is necessary is the social worker's capacity
to reconsider his ethical inclinations when confronting an
ethical issue in his practice, to a sufficient extent at least to
take into account all the factors associated with his ethical
responsibility, or as many of them as he can generate some
awareness and concern about.

Cultural, social, religious, emotional, and other influences do affect the social worker's behavior in relation to
his client, but social work ethics requires disciplined and
rational action responses that are maximally related to his
professional responsibility. His ethical choices should
become rational choices, studiously calculated to maximize
his service to his client, limit his advantage over the client,
and minimize the risks for the client. They are moves based
on his conception of his professional function and on his
awareness of both the practical and the dynamic risks for
the client and for others as they are affected by his action
choices.

The social worker's prospective and actual choices that
affect his ethical as well as his professional obligations toward his client require more deliberateness than spontaneity because, aside from his responsibility to perform a
professional function—which itself implies the studied use
of professional knowledge and skill acquired through
study, training, and experience—the social worker is constantly faced with the need to act on matters affecting,
among other things, the client's material or personal circumstances; the client's revelations and other exposures
that are a function of the social work service situation itself;
the social worker's personal effect on the client, and so on.

The social worker's action choices must be thought through and selected from alternatives of which he is scrupulously aware, and they must be maximally related to his professional function and the ethical risks attendant thereto (Levy, 1972b).

The regulation of the social worker's ethics cannot be left to professional associations and legal mechanisms alone, although these are necessary and must be helped to work as well as they can. Perhaps the most strategic medium of control is the social worker himself, with such reinforcement as may be effected through professional education, socialization, and other professional influences. If society does not succeed, through its own media of control, in finding "ways of manufacturing conscience [Borgatta & Meyer, 1959, p. 15]," the social work profession must help the social worker to create his own. The ethical responsibilities reviewed in the foregoing pages may essentially depend on the individual conscience of the social worker himself.

Socialization through professional education and association with peers can be very important in the development of the social worker's ethical conscience (this construction is less tautological than it looks) for, as Talcott Parsons (1951) indicated in his discussion of the relationship of socialization and social control and the allocative processes of social systems:

> The allocation of personnel between roles in the social system and the socialization processes of the individual are clearly *the same processes* viewed in different perspectives. Allocation is the process seen in the perspective of functional significance to the social system as a system. Socialization on the other hand is the process seen in terms of motivation of the individual actor. Learning to decide between alternatives of role-incumbency which the social system leaves open to the individual is certainly part of social learning and such decisions manifest the value-orientations acquired through socialization. The process of allocation of facilities and re-

wards on the other hand is from the motivational point of view a process of acquisition and loss of valued object-relations by individual actors [p. 207].

Professional education is obviously a strategic medium of socialization—or can be, although it often is not.[2]

[2]Compare Lamborn (1963), who reaches a pessimistic conclusion about contemporary education for professional ethics in American law schools, although it would be surprising if the Watergate affair did not do something to improve that situation (see, for example, Oelsner, 1973a, b, and Goldstein, 1974).

Chapter 19

EDUCATION FOR SOCIAL WORK
ETHICS

In *The Talmud,* that extraordinary repository of ethics and other guides to human conduct, an incident is narrated in which three rabbis debated the question of which is more important, study or practice. Rabbi Tarfon maintained that practice is more important. Rabbi Akiba insisted that study is more important. "Whereupon they all spoke up and said, 'Study is more important, for study leads to practice.' "

In social work education, study *is* practice, and practice requires study. Practice is an integral part of the social work curriculum (Johnson, 1955, p. 68). In fact, social work ethics becomes a part of the social work student's educational experience from the time he applies to the school of social work until he graduates (Faith, 1961).

The problem of inculcating professional ethics through professional education persists and is shared by professional schools in general, with some doubt about the adequacy of current instruction (McGlothlin, 1960, Chap. 8).

Implicit in the concern about the learning and teaching of social work ethics is the probable need for change in students to the extent that their personality or cultural and experiential background has affected their behavior patterns (Howard Bacal, 1972).

The major challenge in the learning and teaching of social work ethics is the ability to tolerate and endure uncertainty in the interest of an "enthusiastic and adventurous curiosity about some of the biggest question marks in our professional field," as Whitehorn (1963, p. 119), put it in relation to medicine and as is true of social work and social work education.

The objective is not to equivocate about social work ethics and about the values on which it is premised, but to open the door of the student's mind to those factors bearing on the ethical issues confronted in social work practice so that the student will consider them adequately before choosing a course of action. The very nature of the student's educational experience should reflect the humility, contemplation, sensitivity—yes, even torment—that may be necessary before the student can feel confident that he has thought about everything he can think of, and done all that he can do, in fulfilling his ethical responsibility in his work and in his relationships to clients, colleagues, employer, society, and anyone or anything else that might be affected by his action or inaction.

Education for social work ethics is thus not a simple matter of indoctrinating students with a few ethical principles that can be readily enunciated and learned by rote, but a complex one of engaging students in the struggle for clarity, conviction, and commitment in relation to ethical responsibility and its prerequisite concern, compassion, and comprehension.

Because social work is a disciplined way of achieving specified ends and is thus guided by consensually adopted values, provision must be made in the curriculum of social work schools for the incorporation by students of these values and for socialization into the behavioral norms these values imply. As an "orderly" procedure or process and a "systematic way" or manner of doing anything, which method is defined to be (Random House Dictionary of the English Language), social work is learned by the student through academic courses and field instruction—that is, supervised practice in a social agency. These relate both to the hows of social work practice and to the background considerations and dynamics that affect practice.

Social work is not so "orderly" or "systematic" a method, however, that it limits the practitioner's judgment concerning the relevance of values to his interventions as a social worker. Very often in fact, the orderliness of his practice is subordinated by professional prescription to values affecting his clients, his colleagues, his agency, his community, his society, and himself.[1] Therefore, these values must become an integral part of the social work student's professional armamentarium if he is to become an ethical as well as a competent practitioner—one whose professional behavior consistently reflects, and is considerate of the values accepted by the social work profession as predominant and fundamental.

Since these values are pervasive in their operation and affect all aspects of social work practice, especially its ethics, they are apt to figure in, or be relevant to all aspects of the social work curriculum. Opportunity for contending with them, at least, is likely to be afforded in virtually all the courses in the curriculum and certainly in field instruction (Pumphrey, 1959). The opportunity may not be exploited, of course, but value and ethical issues are inevitably joined

[1]Pumphrey (1959) defines value as "a usual preference for certain means, ends, and conditions of life, often being accompanied by strong feelings [p. 23]." These preferences may, of course, be positive or negative. Compare Kaufman (1958, pp. 132–133).

in field instruction practice and in social work practice courses. They are no doubt equally irresistible in social welfare, social planning, administration, and other courses. Therefore, special courses in values and ethics may not be absolutely necessary. But whether special courses are arranged or not, some systematization of objectives, content, and learning experiences is necessary if students are not to learn about values and ethics entirely by chance—the chance of relevant classroom and field experience, and the chance of awareness and use of these by students and teachers. A curriculum may be proposed for insuring content in social work values and ethics in all phases and parts of social work education, including special courses that are specifically designed for dealing with it. Special courses are not to be viewed as carrying exclusive responsibility for such content, however; whether they are offered or not, issues in values and ethics should be sought, suggested, and dealt with wherever they occur in the social work curriculum. They are bound to be inescapable in most curriculum areas unless teachers and students alike insist on being blind to them.

The educational objectives affecting social work values and ethics in the social work curriculum include cognitive, conative, emotional, and behavioral ones. Students should be helped, encouraged, and inspired to learn about social work values and ethics so that they become aware of them and aim to realize and implement them in their own practice and in the practices of social institutions. Students should be helped to feel compelled to apply social work values in their own practice and to influence social institutions to apply them. They should also be helped to feel compelled to appreciate the nature of ethical as well as competent social work practice and to develop the capacity to engage in such practice.

Not only should the students' behavior change as a consequence of learning experiences in this connection, but their very will to change should be affirmatively affected. Students should be influenced not only to want to know what values are relevant to professional situations and conflicts that they are likely to experience, but to want to be able to do something about them, whether these values emerge from their job responsibility or from their identification with the social work profession. Students should have the opportunity in both classes and field instruction to suffer the discomfort of uncertainty with respect to the ethical choices they must make, and of inner and outer tension with respect to the consequences of the ethical choices they will have made.

Students should be given the opportunity—through lectures, discussions, reading, role playing, practice, and other learning media—to know what the social work values consensually are; which value issues require resolution or consensus; what the operational effects of these values are at various levels of social structure and organization, from individual client through family, groups, committees, and community on up to society in some large collective sense; what behavioral expectations these values connote; how one proceeds to reckon with conflicts among them and priorities affecting them; and how one makes systematic and well-founded choices of ethical intervention in the face of contradictory considerations affecting clients, significant others, agency, community, and society.

Thus educational objectives concerning values and ethics include what students—in the judgment of faculty, with some influence and help from the social work profession and social work practice in general—ought to know; what they ought to feel about what they know, what they ought to do about what they know, and what responsibility they ought to share with professional peers when attempting to resolve issues concerning social work values and ethics that emerge in social work practice generally, and affect and concern the social work profession as a whole.

Learning experiences for students in relation to values

and ethics derive from the content deemed best to represent values and ethics. Therefore, the first step in planning
learning experiences for social work students is to identify
values that are regarded as relevant to students' beginning
competence as social workers and to their ethics. These
values would include those already codified in the code of
ethics, professional policy statements, and other accredited
documents and literature that have been endorsed by professional groups and associations such as the National Association of Social Workers; the Council on Social Work
Education; and the local, national and international stan-
dard-setting bodies of the various fields of practice. These
values would also include those that remain in contention,
the analysis and contemplation of which may contribute to
learning, if not about the values themselves, then about the
manner in which their relevance to practice and social action situations can be weighed and in which the appropriateness of their application can be appraised.

These values represent the conceptions of people, the
outcomes for people, and the instruments for dealing with
people proposed by the collectivity of the social work profession in relation both to social work practice and to social
conditions (Levy, 1973e). Particular values can be selected
and emphasized, depending on the context in which they
will be considered—as in particular courses, the field instruction setting, and so forth—and on the stage of the
social work education program in which they will be considered. But values can also be more flexibly considered in
relation to the students' readiness to deal with them and in
relation to what appears to be pertinent in the light of the
students' contemporary needs and experience. Current
events and issues, both in the field instruction practice of
students and in the community and world around them,
may also serve as a salutary influence (and a meaningful
one for the students) on the selection of values for classroom and supervisory analysis.

Having identified the values that merit consideration

and incorporation by students, instructors would, as the second step, then formulate them into teaching-practice content, shaped into forms that most closely relate to what students are doing in classes and the field and what they are most likely to have a pressing need for. Thus the dignity of the individual may be identified as a value to which social workers subscribe and to which they are agreed to be committed in their practice. But that is a general expression of the value: one that is applicable in almost any context. For the social work student, it attains pertinence to social work as the meaning of dignity is explored in the light of clients' need for help, their conditions, and their powerlessness— especially in relation to the relatively advantageous position of the social worker and the institution that clients resort to for help, at times in spite of themselves. So formulated, the identified value becomes a value in the professional context. It is not only the value that then impresses the social work student as important; also significant for him is *why* it is important in relation to his practice.

As the third step in planning learning experiences for students in relation to values and ethics, instructors would translate the identified values into learning, teaching, and practice processes. This step represents the conceptualization of the values for practice purposes and their readiness for application in practice. Having established their professional context and their import within that context, instructors would translate the values into terms connected with students' experiences. For example, what does the dignity of the individual mean to the student when he is in eyeball-to-eyeball confrontation with a client? What does it mean when the student is not professionally exposed to a particular group or class of persons but is aware of their miserable condition that leaves them devoid of dignity?

And finally, though not exhaustively, instructors would consider how they will represent the identified values: the role they will play in making them vivid and urgent as content for social work education, and the means they will use, whether through records, assignments, post-mortem supervisory review, or whatever, to see that the values and the ethical principles that flow from them are articulated. Not excluded would be the actual way in which instructors relate to and deal with students, which is sometimes more of an indicator of a given value's place in the professional life of the instructor than the most erudite exegesis on it.

Since knowledge in social work and social work education is knowledge for use, students' knowledge about values is reflected not only in their oral and written communications but in their behavior with reference to those values. Because ethics is essentially values in action, content with respect to identified values would therefore include what students would do and actually do with reference to the values. That which is professionally preferred —as conceptions of persons, outcomes for them, or instruments of practice with them—is expected to be acted on. Students may be given the opportunity to act on values, to be confronted with or to consider actions based on them, and perhaps—if the values have already been discovered and identified—to be helped to derive principles of value-based action. If the values have not yet been discovered and identified, students may be challenged to discover and identify them, and to propose action principles based on them.

Professional ethics represents idealizations of behavior—that is, judgments concerning what is "right" and "good" in professional conduct and the conduct of professional practitioners. Students could therefore be given the opportunity to test their behavioral responses in professional situations, either by way of anticipation or by way of retrospective analysis, so that the reasonably evident principles of "right" conduct can be identified and conceptually crystallized, and so that the principles that are paradoxical under given circumstances can be brooded over and reconsidered. A challenge that can be productive for students is the determination of whether a deviation from ethical or idealized conduct—for example, depriving a client of autonomy, or depriving one group of equal opportunity in employment or service to accord preferential treatment to another—is but a rare and justifiable exception (the idealization otherwise remaining intact), or a cloud on the idealization itself.

In summary, then, a plan for dealing with values and ethics in social work education requires (1) the identification of values that are important for students to master and act on; (2) the selection of those values that students will be given the opportunity to consider; (3) the formulation and translation of the selected values into a form that makes evident and imperative their relevance to social work and to students' practice; and (4) the contemplation of the means and experiences through which students will be given the opportunity to master the selected values and reflect them in their practice, and the contemplation of the way instructors will use themselves in the process. An additional step to be provided for is that of evaluation. The purpose of evaluation is to appraise students' achievements in the realm of social work values and ethics. The educational problem is to determine whether students have incorporated the values and ethics of their profession sufficiently and appropriately to be ethical practitioners, oriented not only to the values of the social work profession but also to the value of free and constant inquiry into them.

Unlike curriculum content which is more cognitively oriented, content in social work values and ethics is apt to generate an intense emotional charge, especially if these values and ethics differ from the values and ethical principles to which students have been previously committed. Social work students may, in fact, face conflicts of crisis proportions when they begin to suspect that faculty and field instructors expect of them what they regard as revolutionary and even undesirable change. Changing their values and ethics is difficult for students—particularly when a given mode of thinking and behaving is deeply ingrained in them, as values and ethics are likely to be. Students are almost certain to perceive such a change as integral to the professional development that faculty and field instructors are pressing on them. Bias and preoccupation on the part of faculty and field instructors are not likely to escape students notice. Therefore, they are bound to conclude that satisfactory fulfillment of school requirements will be impossible unless they give evidence of the necessary change in their values and ethics. And they are bound to experience great strain when the professional orientation to values and ethics that appears to guide faculty and field instructors is, in some respect, alien to them. This is undoubtedly one of the "special stresses in social work learning" that, according to Charlotte Towle (1954, p. 63), leads to the prominent operation of the student's "protective function." For "the protective function to operate in the interest of integration and execution," faculty and field instructors must help social work students shift the basis of their aspirations for learning from those that are purely protective to those that are more clearly developmental.

Learning, in other words, may represent for the social work student a means of self-preservation, accommodation, or professional development based on professional ideals and service objectives. Self-preservation is designed by the student to help him escape penalties such as failure; accommodation, to help him reap approval; and professional development, to help him to achieve mastery. The first is most resistive to real change. The second is a show of change for the purpose of managing a situation and authoritative persons. The resulting behavior, as in a revised value or in ethical behavior in a practice situation, is genuine enough but is sometimes limited in durability because it is conditioned by the immediate goal of satisfying a particular situation, a particular person, or both. One can have only limited confidence that the student will achieve a similar result once he has left the school and the person with authority, such as the faculty member or field instructor. Learning that takes place in response to the quest for professional development—the quest for ethical performance and for mastery of the principles that can be called on to achieve it—is more durable. It does not depend on the particular setting and the particular persons who are overseeing it. It does not depend on the fear of failing a course or field instruction, nor does it depend on the fear of loss of the teacher's or field instructor's approval. It depends rather on the student's zeal to be helpful and ethical as a social worker, and to rely increasingly on his own knowledge, feelings, and resources to do so.

The student's view of success is not a high grade or an authoritative pat on his back but objective evidence of value-based and ethical practice, with full awareness of what made it so and with full confidence that he can replicate the process and has the will to do it.

The source of the student's learning in the other instances is external: it is outer-directed. The source of the student's learning in the quest for professional development is internal: both the reason for it and its nature are inner-directed. Changes in students' professional values and ethics for application in social work practice, when indicated, are not truly attested to unless and until they have become inner-directed. Since such changes are rarely more than beginnings in social work education—certainly at the master's level and below, and certainly with respect to values and ethics that embrace the very personalities of students—the nature of the learning process is as significant as the learning that appears to take place, because the school must rely on the student's capacity for continued change, growth, and development after graduation.

All this suggests that teachers and field instructors must be concerned not only about what students are learning about social work values and ethics but about how they are learning it. The articulation of values and ethics is not unimportant, but neither is it sufficient for evidence of mastery. For this purpose, students need opportunities to distinguish between the analysis of needs, situations, and professional practice in relation to the service and social outcomes sought and the analysis of the value and ethical issues that affect them. Teachers and field instructors must sensitize students to the difference and afford them opportunities to cope with the difference. This is particularly important when a conflict of action choice or consequence results from or is implicit in the difference. For example, students who are engaged in a theoretical or actual confrontation with a case involving an abused child need the opportunity to consider the practice implications of perceiving the parents as well as the child as clients; but they also need the opportunity to contend with the value and ethical implications of dealing with both, and with the law and the agency's function at the same time. What is regarded as effective for both children and parents in terms of practice approaches, must be set alongside what is valued for both and what is owed to each as well as others. Students need the opportunity to contend with the ethical conflicts that are apt to color the concurrent valuation of independence and interdependence; client well-being and societal well-being; client and significant others; autonomy and social responsibility; responsibility to agency and professional responsibility; clients and colleagues; and so on.

Teachers and field instructors do not have to feel compelled to provide answers, but they must raise questions or generate them in students, for the objective is not simply to enunciate values or prescribe ethical responses but to help students to apply them, derive them, formulate them, and refine them for future use in a variety of situations. The objective is also to solidify them as a basis for students' socialization into the social work profession, for their identification with the profession, and for their sense of responsibility in relation to it and its role in society.

As already intimated, the behavior of teachers and field instructors—in classes, in the school, in agencies, and in the community—can also be a significant influence on what students learn about social work values and ethics. The objective, however, is not to stimulate imitative conceptualization and behavior, but to inspire ideals, to reinforce salutary professional inclinations, and to promote introspection and inquiry. The message is not "Be like me" but "There are professional reasons why I feel I must do what I do. Consider them. Question them. Test them. Come to your own terms with them."

Social work is a value-based profession. It is not only a way of doing something, but a constellation of preferences concerning what merits doing and how it should be done. It is suffused with idealistic aspirations for people and idealistic notions about how people should be treated. Its practitioners are surcharged with behavioral expectations. Social workers may not be perfect, or even seem perfect to the clients they work with as well as others who are aware of them or are exposed to them, but practices and concerns that are not expected of ordinary mortals are expected of them. They are far from all-powerful, but most people expect them to be "fair and square" until they are proved otherwise.

This is but a composite approximation of social work and social workers which is shared by social workers and non-social workers alike, and one that generally represents the station of social work and social workers in modern life. There can therefore be no doubt about either the place of values and ethics in the social work curriculum or the urgency of dealing with them effectively if social work and social workers of the future are to fit the approximation and, by their ethical practice, validate and embellish it.

Chapter 20

PROBLEMS, PROSPECTS, AND DILEMMAS

Although the foregoing presents some basis for social workers' intelligent and compassionate contention with ethical issues in social work practice, and for educational preparation for the process, it does leave a substantial residue of problems and dilemmas. Many of them have already been alluded to. The fact that the social worker has concurrent ethical responsibility in a number of directions, frequently involving irreconcilable interests, is but one of the bases for conflict and at times irresolution. There are many others.

The problem of uncertainty may well be an inspiration to inquiry if a social worker can overcome his zeal for dogma and his penchant for oversimplification. But it can also be a stimulus to despair in a social work service situation. The social worker may "want to act *rightly,* ethically and constructively," but how is he "to know whether his action is 'right.' " Who is so "all-wise" and "all-knowing" [Kuenzli, 1959]?"

There is always the danger of role-confusion, "so seductive to the educated", as Pellegrino (1963) has said, which subjects social workers to the temptation to assert "authority and prerogatives outside the domain of one's competence [p. 19]." Katkin (1972), for example, has identified a number of legal hazards that may be associated with the practitioner's inclination to be humane, and to feel professionally equipped as well as authorized to do so. Injustices have sometimes resulted for clients whom social workers have presumed to protect. Such injustices have been avoided only when the courts have attended to the legal rights of clients.

The nature of the social work service situation compels the conclusion that the burden of proof of ethical conduct is on the social worker. More affirmatively, social work ethics, while serving as a guide for action choices in relation to ethical issues, also serves as a basis for expectations and predictions (compare Lundberg, 1948). This suggests a particular problem for the social work profession because many kinds of persons do many kinds of social work in many kinds of places.

There is no guarantee that the professionally educated social worker will inevitably be ethical, or at least contend thoroughly with ethical issues in the attempt to be as ethical as he possibly can. But at least one can assume that through social work education and supervision, he has been exposed to concern about his ethics and to opportunities to learn how to act on this concern. What about the social worker who lacks professional education, however? He may, of course, be as ethical as any professionally educated social worker, but what basis is there for confidence that he will be? There must be a glimmer of doubt about the prospect of ethical conduct, for example, on the part of the so-called indigenous nonprofessional or paraprofessional social worker and perhaps the minimally educated social work student (e.g., one who has completed an associate degree or undergraduate educational program in social work).

This doubt is only reinforced by "the use of people with a problem to help other people who have the same problem in more severe form [Riessman, 1965, p. 27]." True, such "helpers" may benefit from their role, and they are entitled to consideration in relation to their own needs. But is this a justifiable medium in view of the ethical responsibility that is owed to clients?[1] "A person in a 'helping' profession must learn the discipline of responding to the client's needs rather than to his own. The art of practice combines knowledge, skill, and self [McGlothlin, 1960, p. 113]."

The employment of indigenous nonprofessionals in some social agencies and programs has been justified on the basis of their special capacity to help others with whom they have a natural rapport because they share characteristics, language, experience, or problems. Undoubtedly these people have performed useful and creditable functions. But, issues of competence and knowledge aside, the question remains whether they come with a sufficient orientation to social work ethics to be consistently disciplined in its application. Some kind of compensation for this possible deficiency would seem necessary if the alternative of exclusion is not to be found acceptable.

All in all, then, social work ethics, necessary as it is, is also not without its difficulties. As a final note, we can do no better than recall the words of the late Earl Warren (1962), former chief justice of the United States, which, although not addressed to social work or social work ethics have a ring of immediate relevance to them:

[1]Gans (1962) identified some of the critical limitations of nonprofessional helping persons or "internal caretakers" that, from the perspective of ethical responsibility, introduce many doubts and reservations. Riessman (1963) offered a more optimistic view.

In the Law beyond the Law, which calls upon us to be fair in business, where the Law cannot command fairness; which bids us temper justice with mercy, where the Law can only enforce justice; which demands our compassion for the unfortunate, although the Law can only give him his legal due, each of us is necessarily his own Chief Justice. In fact, he is the whole Supreme Court, from which there lies no appeal. The individual citizen may engage in practices which, on the advice of counsel, he believes strictly within the letter of the Law but which he also knows from his own conscience are outside the bounds of propriety and the right. Thus, when he engages in such practices, he does so not at his own peril —as when he violates the Law—but at peril to the structure of civilization, involving greater stakes than any possible peril to himself.

REFERENCES

Abbott, T. K. (Trans.) *Kant's critique of practical reason and other works on the theory of ethics.* (4th ed.) London: Longmans, Green, 1889.

Adams, M. L., & Berman, D. C. The hospital through a child's eyes. *Children,* **12**(3), 1965, 102–104.

Addams, J. *Twenty years at Hull House.* New York: New American Library, 1961.

Addams, J. *Democracy and social ethics.* Edited by A. F. Scott. Cambridge, Mass.: Harvard University Press, Belknap Press, 1964.

Allen, F. H. The dilemma of growth. *Archives of Neurology and Psychiatry,* **37**, 1937, 859–869.

American Association of Social Workers. Standards for the professional practice of social work, adopted by the 1951 delegate assembly. Supplement to *Social Work Journal,* July 1952, Part II.

American Psychological Association. *Ethical standards of psychologists.* Washington, D.C.: A.P.A., 1953.

American Steel Foundries v. *Tri-City Central Trades Council,* 257 U.S. 189 (1921)

Aptekar, H. H. The significance of dependence and independence in supervision. *Social Casework,* **35**(6), 1954, 238–245.

Aptekar, H. H. Supervision and the development of professional responsibility: An application of systems thought. *Jewish Social Work Forum,* **3**(1), 1965, 4–17.

Babcock, C. G. Social work as work. *Social Casework,* **34**(10), 1953, 415–422.

Bacal, H. A. Balint groups: Training or treatment? *Psychiatry in Medicine,* **3**(4), 1972, 373–377.

Baker v. *Humphrey,* 101 U.S. 494 (1879).

Barber, B. Some problems in the sociology of the professions. *Daedalus,* **92**(4), 1963, 669–688.

Barkan, T. W. Private casework practice in a medical clinic. *Social Work,* **18**(4), 1973, 5–9.

Barry, B. *Political argument.* London: Routledge & Kegan Paul, 1965.

Bartlett, H. M. Toward clarification and improvement of social work practice. *Social Work,* **3**(2), 1958, 3–5. (a)

Bartlett, H. M. Working definition of social work practice. *Social Work,* **3**(2) 1958, 5–9. (b)

Begelman, D. A. The ethics of behavioral control and a new mythology. *Psychotherapy: Theory, Research and Practice,* **8**(2), 1971, 165–169.

Benoit-Smullyan, E. Status, status types, and status interrelations. *American Sociological Review,* **9**(2), 1944, 151–161.

Berg, B. R. Transference and the camp counselor. *Social Casework,* **31**(5), 1950, 201–204.

Bernstein, S. Self-determination: King or citizen in the realm of values? *Social Work,* **5**(1), 1960, 3–8.

Berton, P. *The comfortable pew.* Toronto: McClelland & Stewart, 1965.

Biestek, F. P. The principle of client self-determination. *Social Casework,* **32**(9), 1951, 369–375.

Black's Law Dictionary. (3rd ed.) St. Paul, Minn.: West Publishing, 1933.

Blau, P. M. *Exchange and power in social life.* New York: John Wiley, 1964.

Blau, P. M., & Scott, R. W. *Formal organizations: A comparative approach.* San Francisco: Chandler, 1962.

Blauch, L. E. (Ed.) *Education for the professions.* Washington, D.C.: U.S. Department of Health, Education, & Welfare, 1955.

Blaustein, A. P., Porter, C. O., & Duncan, C. T. *The American lawyer: A summary of the survey of the legal profession.* Chicago: University of Chicago Press, 1954.

Bohem, W. W. The nature of social work. *Social Work*, **3**(2), 1958, 10–18.

Bonhoeffer, D. *Ethics.* Edited by E. Bethage, translated by N. H. Smith. London: Fontana Library, 1964.

Borgatta, E. F., & Meyer, H. J. (eds.) *Social control and the foundations of sociology: Pioneer contributions of Edward Alsworth Ross to the study of society.* Boston: Beacon Press, 1959.

Boudreau, P. J. *Survey of the Canadian Association of Social Workers* (a study of the membership of the Canadian Association with special reference to the attitudes of the membership toward regulation of the social work profession). (Master's research report, School of Social Work, University of Toronto) Toronto, Ontario, Canada, 1965.

Brager, G. A. Institutional change: Perimeters of the possible. *Social Work,* **12**(1), 1967, 59–69.

Brand, G. E. *Bar associations, attorneys and judges: Organization, ethics and discipline.* Chicago: American Judicature Society, 1956.

Breggin, P. R. Coercion of voluntary patients in an open hospital. *Archives of General Psychiatry,* **10**, 1964, 173–177.

Brown, J. M. Power. In J. Gould & W. L. Kolb (Eds.), *A dictionary of the social sciences.* London: Tavistock, 1964.

Bugental, J. F. The person who is the psychotherapist. *Journal of Counseling Psychology,* **27**, 1964, 272–277.

Caplan, G. Introduction and overview. In Caplan (Ed.), *Prevention of mental disorders in children: Initial explorations.* New York: Basic Books, 1961.

Carey, J. L., & Doherty, W. D. The concept of independence—review and restatement. *Journal of Accountancy,* 1966, 38–48.

Carlin, J. E. *Lawyer's ethics.* New York: Russell Sage Foundation, 1966.

Carr-Saunders, A. M., & Wilson, P. A. *The professions.* London: Frank Cass, 1964. (Reprinted from 1933 edition.)

Cloward, R. A., & Elman, R. M. Poverty, injustice and the welfare state, Parts 1 & 2. *Nation,* February 28, 1966, 230–235, and March 7, 1966, 264–268.

Code of ethics and its implementation (Editorial). *The Social Worker (Le Travailleur Social),* **34**(2), 1966, 76–77.

Cohen, M. The emergence of private practice in social work. *Social Problems,* **14**(1), 1966, 84–93.

Cohen, M. R. *Reason and law.* New York: Collier Books, 1961.

Commercial Merchant's National Bank and Trust Co. et al. v. *Kloth et al.,* 360 Ill. 294, 196 N.E. 214 (1935).

Council of the Institute of Chartered Accountants in England and Wales. Accountants' liability to Third Parties: The Hedley Byrne Decision. *The Accountant,* **153**(4729), 1965, 163–164.

Croxton-Smith, C. Professional ethics. *Accountancy,* **76**(864), 1965, 749–757. (a)

Croxton-Smith, C. Professional ethics—III. *The Accountant,* **153**(4731), 1965, 240–247. (b)

Daniels, A. K. The captive professional: Bureaucratic limitations in the practice of military psychiatry. *Journal of Health and Social Behavior,* **10**(4), 1969, 255–265.

Dean, E. S. Writing psychiatric reports. *American Journal of Psychiatry,* **119** (8), 1963, 759–762.

Dembo, T. The utilization of psychological knowledge in rehabilitation. *Welfare in Review,* **8**(4), 1970, 1–7.

Deutsch, A. American labor and social work. *Science and Society,* **8**(4), 1944, 289–304.

Developments in the law: Equal protection. *Harvard Law Review,* **82**(5), 1969, 1065–1192.

Diesing, P. *Reason in society.* Urbana: University of Illinois Press, 1962.

Dostoevsky, F. M. Notes from underground. In W. Kaufmann (Ed. and trans.), *Existentialism from Dostoevsky to Sartre.* Cleveland: World Publishing, 1956.

Drucker, R. & King, D. Private practice services for low income people (Brief Notes). *Social Work,* **18**(2), 1973, 115, 117–118.

Durkheim, E. *Professional ethics and civic morals.* Translated by C. Brookfield. Glencoe, Ill.: Free Press, 1958.

Edel, A. Anthropology and ethics in common focus. *Journal of the Royal Anthropological Institute,* **92** (Part 1), 1962, 55–72.

Edel, A. *Method in ethical theory.* Indianapolis: Bobbs-Merrill, 1963.

Edman, I. (Ed.) *The works of Plato.* Jowett translation. New York: Modern Library, 1956.

Ehrlich, J. W. *Ehrlich's Blackstone.* New York: Capricorn Books, 1959.

Emerson, R. M. Power-dependency relations. *American Sociological Review,* **27**(1), 1962, 31–41.

Epstein, L. Is autonomous practice possible? *Social Work,* **18**(2), 1973, 5–12.

Erikson, E. H. *Childhood and society.* (2nd ed.) New York: W. W. Norton, 1963.

Faith, G. B. Ethics and values intrinsic to teaching and learning in the first year of professional education in social work. (Position paper, Workshop 9, *Inclusion of value and ethical content in the social work curriculum.*) Annual program meeting, Council on Social Work Education) Montreal, Canada, 1961. Mimeographed.

Feinberg, J. Supererogation and rules. *Ethics,* **71**(4), 1961, 276–288.

Felix, R. H. The image of the psychiatrist: Past, present and future. *American Journal of Psychiatry,* **121**(4), 1964, 318–322.

Fitch, J. A. Professional workers as trade unionists. Reprint of address presented to the American Federation of State, County and Municipal Employees, AFL–CIO. Washington, D.C.: AFL–CIO, 1950.

Flexner, A. Is social work a profession? *Proceedings of the National Conference of Charities and Corrections,* 1915. Chicago: Hildmann Printing, 1915, 576–590.

Frame, D. M. (Trans.) *The complete works of Montaigne.* Stanford, Calif.: Stanford University Press, 1957.

Fried, C. *An anatomy of values: Problems of personal and social choice.* Cambridge, Mass.: Harvard University Press, 1970.

Fromm-Reichmann, F. *Principles of intensive psychotherapy.* Chicago: University of Chicago Press, 1950.

Gans, H. *The urban villagers.* Glencoe, Ill.: Free Press, 1962.

Garner, H. H. A confrontation technique used in psychotherapy. *Comprehensive Psychiatry,* **1**(4), 1960, 201–211.

Garner, H. H., & Jeans, R. F. Confrontation technique in psychotherapy: Some existential implications. *Journal of Existential Psychiatry,* **11**(8), 1962, 393–408.

Geist, G. O., Curin, S., Prestridge, R., & Schleb, G. Ethics and the counselor-agency relationship. *Rehabilitation Counseling Bulletin,* **17**(1), 1973, 15–21.

Ginsburg, S. W. *A psychiatrist's views on social issues.* New York: Columbia University Press, 1963.

Goldberg, A. J. Civil rights in labor-management relations: A labor viewpoint. *Annals of the American Academy of Political and Social Science,* **275**, May 1951, 148–154.

Goldberg, J. R. The professional and his union in the Jewish center. *Journal of Jewish Communal Service,* **36**(3), 1960, 284–289.

Goldhamer, H., & Shils, E. A. Types of power and status. *American Journal of Sociology,* **45**(2), 1939, 171–182.

Goldstein, T. Watergate stirs new look at lawyers' self-policing. *New York Times,* May 29, 1974.

Golton, M. A. Private practice in social work. *Encyclopedia of Social Work.* New York: National Association of Social Workers, 1971.

Goode, W. J. Community within a community: The professions. *American Sociological Review,* **22**(2) 1957, 194–200.

Greenwood, E. Attributes of a profession. *Social Work,* **2**(3), 1957, 45–55.

Grossbard, H. Methodology for developing self-awareness. *Social Casework,* **35**(9), 1954, 380–386.

Grosser, G. H., & Paul, N. L. Ethical issues in family group therapy. *American Journal of Orthopsychiatry,* **34**(5), 1964, 875–894.

Grossman, D. Ego-activating approaches to psychotherapy. *Psycho-Analytic Review,* **51**(3), 1964, 65–88.

Grotjohn, M. Psychoanalysis and faith: The thirty-year debate between Sigmund Freud and Oskar Pfister. In S. C. Post (Ed.), *Moral values and the superego concept in psychoanalysis.* New York: International Universities Press, 1972.

Group for the Advancement of Psychiatry, Committee on Psychiatry and Law. *Confidentiality and privileged communication in the practice of psychiatry,* Report No. 45. New York: G.A.P., June, 1960.

Grygier, T. Crime and society. In W. G. McGrath (Ed.), *Crime and its treatment in Canada.* Toronto: Macmillan, 1965.

Grygier, T. The concept of the "state of delinquency"—an obituary. Unpublished manuscript, University of Toronto School of Social Work, undated.

Guest editorial. *Social Work,* **7**(3), 1962, 2, 128.

Hackbusch, F. Professional ethics in institution practice. *American Psychologist,* **3**(3), 1948, 85–87.

Haefner, A. E. The ethical syllogism. *Ethics,* **71**(4), 1961, 289–295.

Hailman, D. E. A code of ethics for the social worker. *Social Work Journal,* **30**(2), 1949, 44–50.

Haley, J. *Strategies of psychotherapy.* New York: Grune & Stratton, 1963.

Hall, L. K. Group workers and professional ethics. *The Group,* **15**(1), 1952, 3–8.

Hall, O. The place of the professions in the urban community. In S. D. Clark (Ed.), *Urbanism and the changing Canadian society.* Toronto: University of Toronto Press, 1961.

Halleck, S. L. The impact of professional dishonesty on behavior of disturbed adolescents. *Social Work,* **8**(2), 1963, 48–56.

Hamilton, G. Self-awareness in professional education. *Social Casework,* **35**(9), 1954, 371–379.

Hartmann, H. *Psychoanalysis and moral values.* New York: International Universities Press, 1960.

Haug, M. R., & Sussman, M. B. Professional autonomy and the revolt of the client. *Social Problems,* **17**(2), 1969, 153–161.

Hegel. *Encyclopedia of Philosophy.* Translated and annotated by G. E. Mueller. New York: Philosophical Library, 1959.

Hofstein, S. The nature of process: Its implications for social work. *Journal of Social Work Process,* Vol. **14**. Philadelphia: University of Pennsylvania Press, 1964.

Hollender, M. H. Privileged communication and confidentiality. *Diseases of the Nervous System,* **26**(3), 1965, 169–175.

Hollis, F. *Casework: A psycho-social therapy.* New York: Random House, 1964.

Horsburgh, H. J. N. Trust and social objectives. *Ethics,* **72**(1), 1961, 28–40.

Hughes, E. C. *Men and their work.* Glencoe, Ill.: Free Press, 1958.

Hunter, F. *Community power structure: A study of decision makers.* Chapel Hill: University of North Carolina Press, 1953.

Ilan, E. The problem of motivation in the educator's vocational choice. *Psychoanalytic Study of the Child,* Vol. 18. New York: International Universities Press, 1963.

In re Farmer, 191 N.C. 235, 131 S.E. 661 (1926).

In re Soale, 31 Cal. App. 144, 159 P. 1065 (1916).

Johnson, A. Educating professional social workers for ethical practice. In *Education for Social Work 1955.* New York: Council on Social Work Education, 1955.

Jones, W. H. S. (Trans.) Appendix to W. T. Fitts, Jr., & B. Fitts, Ethical standards of the medical profession. *Annals of the American Academy of Political and Social Science,* **297**, January 1955, 17–36.

Kadushin, A. The knowledge base of social work. In A. J. Kahn (Ed.), *Issues in American social work.* New York: Columbia University Press, 1959.

Kahn, R. L. Staff attitudes toward psychiatric treatment in a voluntary mental hospital. *Journal of the Hillside Hospital,* **10**(2), 1961, 97–106.

Kairys, D. The training analysis: A critical review of the literature and a controversial proposal. *Psychoanalytic Quarterly,* **33**(4), 1964. 485–512.

Kant, I. *Lectures on Ethics.* Translated by L. Infield. New York: Harper Torchbook, 1963.

Kantor, R. E. Schizophrenia and the Protestant ethic. *Mental Hygiene,* **50** (1), 1966, 18–23.

Kardiner, A. Security, cultural restraints, intrasocial dependencies, and hostilities. *The Family,* **18**(6), 1937, 183–196.

Katkin, D. Legal and ethical problems related to social work participation in the sentencing of criminal offenders. *Smith College Studies in Social Work,* 42(2), 1972, 146–154.

Katz, H. *Cathedral of humanity: A study of Jane Addams' ideas on art and culture.* (Doctoral dissertation, Wurzweiler School of Social Work, Yeshiva University) New York, N.Y., 1975.

Kaufman, F. *Methodology of the social sciences.* New York: Humanities Press, 1958.

Keith-Lucas, A. A critique of the principle of client self-determination. *Social Work,* **8**(3), 1963, 66–71.

Kleinsasser, D., & Morton, W. D. Treatment ethics: A fine and sometimes elusive line. *Journal of the Fort Logan Mental Health Center,* **5**(1), 1968, 1–20.

Kuenzli, A. E. An objective basis for ethics. Humanist Reprint Series, No. 106. Yellow Springs, Ohio: The American Humanist Association, 1959.

Kusmer, K. L. The functions of organized charity in the progressive era: Chicago as a case study. *The Journal of American History,* **60,** 1973, 657–678.

Lamborn, L. L. *Legal ethics and professional responsibility: (a survey of current methods of instruction in American law schools.* Chicago: American Bar Foundation, 1963.

Lasagna, L. Would Hippocrates rewrite his oath? *New York Times Magazine,* June 28, 1964, 11, 41–43.

Levenstein, S. *Private practice in social casework.* New York: Columbia University Press, 1964.

Levy, C. S. Social action, social work and Jewish social philosophy in Jewish community center practice. *Journal of Jewish Communal Service,* **40**(1), 1963, 124–134. (a)

Levy, C. S. Social worker and client as obstacles to client self-determination. *Journal of Jewish Communal Service,* **39**(4), 1963, 416–419. (b)

Levy, C. S. Labor-management relations in the Jewish community center. *Journal of Jewish Communal Service,* **41**(1), 1964, 114–123.

Levy, C. S. A conceptual framework for field instruction in social work education. *Child Welfare*, **44**(8), 1965, 447–452. (a)

Levy, C. S. When a model is not a model. *Child Welfare*, **44**(2), 1965, 95–99. (b)

Levy, C. S. Community involvement and responsibility. *New York Journal of Medicine*, **68**(17), 1968, 2297–2302.

Levy, C. S. Power through participation: The royal road to social change. *Social Work*, **15**(3), 1970, 105–108.

Levy, C. S. (The graduate) school (of social work) and society. *Journal of Education for Social Work*, **7**(2), 1971, 25–30.

Levy, C. S. The context of social work ethics. *Social Work*, **17**(2), 1972, 95–101. (a)

Levy, C. S. Professional ethics as humanistic ethics. *Jewish Social Work Forum*, **9**(1), 1972, 5–12 (b)

Levy, C. S. Values and planned change. *Social Casework*, **53**(8), 1972, 488–493. (c)

Levy, C. S. *Education and training for the fundraising function*. New York: Bureau for Careers in Jewish Service, 1973. (a)

Levy, C. S. The ethics of supervision. *Social Work*, **18**(2), 1973, 14–21. (b)

Levy, C. S. The social worker as agent of policy change. In E. Manser (Ed.), *Family advocacy: A manual for action*. New York: Family Service Association of America, 1973. (c)

Levy, C. S. Social work's status as a profession: Effect on client autonomy. *Jewish Social Work Forum*, **10**(2), 1973, 4–17. (d)

Levy, C. S. The value base of social work. *Journal of Education for Social Work*, **9**(1), 1973, 34–42. (e)

Levy, C. S. Advocacy and the injustice of justice. *Social Service Review*, **48**(1), 1974, 39–50. (a)

Levy, C. S. Inputs versus outputs as criteria of competence. *Social Casework*, **55**(6), 1974, 375–380. (b)

Levy, C. S. On the development of a code of ethics. *Social Work*, **19**(2), 1974, 207–216. (c)

Levy, C. S. Putting the social work back into social work. *Journal of Jewish Communal Service*, **51**(2), 1974, 171–178. (d)

Levy, C. S. The relevance (or irrelevance) of consequences to social work ethics. *Journal of Jewish Communal Service*, **51**(1), 1974, 73–81. (e)

Lewis, H. Morality and the politics of practice. *Social Casework*, **53**(7), 1972, 404–417.

Lippitt, R., Watson, J., & Westley, B. *The dynamics of planned change.* New York: Harcourt, Brace, 1958.

London, P. *Behavior control.* New York: Harper & Row, Perennial Library, 1971.

Lowe, C. M. Value orientations—an ethical dilemma. *American Psychologist,* **14**(11), 1959, 687–693.

Lowney, P. *Gleeb.* New York: Dodd, Mead, 1973.

Lubove, R. *The professional altruist: The emergence of social work as a career— 1880–1930.* Cambridge, Mass.: Harvard University Press, 1965.

Lund, T. *A guide to the professional conduct and etiquette of solicitors.* London: Law Society, 1960.

Lundberg, G. Semantics and the value problem. Social Forces, **27**(1), 1948, 114–117.

MacIver, R. M. The social significance of professional ethics. *Annals of the American Academy of Political and Social Science,* **297,** January 1955, 118–124.

Malmquist, C. M. Problems of confidentiality in child psychiatry. *American Journal of Orthopsychiatry,* **35**(4), 1965, 787–792.

McCloskey, H. J. Toward an objectivist ethic. *Ethics,* **73**(1), 1962, 10–27.

McGee, C. D. Explicit definitions and ethical rules. *Ethics,* **73(3), 1963, 198–207.**

McGlothlin, W. J. *Patterns of professional education.* New York: Putnam, 1960.

Melden, A. I. *Rights and right conduct.* Oxford, Eng.: Basil Blackwell, 1959.

Merriam, C. E. *A study of power.* Glencoe, Ill.: Free Press, 1950.

Meunier v. *Bernich et al.,* 170 So. 567 (1936).

Miller, A. The price. *The Saturday Evening Post,* February 10, 1968, 40.

Mills, C. W. *White collar.* New York: Oxford University Press, 1956.

Monypenny, P. The control of ethical standards in the public service. *Annals of the American Academy of Political and Social Science,* **297,** January 1955, 98–104.

Murphy, J. G. Law logic. *Ethics,* **77**(3), 1967, 193–198.

Mutter v. *Burgess et al.,* 290 F. 269 (1930).

National Association of Social Workers. *Goals of public social policy.* New York, NASW, 1963.

National Association of Social Workers, Committee on the Study of Competence. Social work competence: Its nature and components. *Personnel Information,* **8**(2), 1965, 1, 33–36.

National Association of Social Workers, Ad Hoc Committee on Advocacy. The social worker as advocate: Champion of social victims. *Social Work,* **14**(2), 1969, 16–22.

National Association of Social Workers, Committee on the Study of Competence. *Guidelines for the assessment of professional competence in social work.* New York: Author, 1972.

National Association of Social Workers, Commission on Social Work Ethics. *The social workers' code of ethics: A critique and guide.* New York: Author, undated. Mimeographed.

National Association of Social Workers. Midnight raids. New York: NASW. Undated brochure.

National Association of Social Workers. Regulation of social work practice. Resolution adopted by the NASW delegate assembly, 1964, Mimeographed.

National Association of Social Workers. *Utilization of personnel in social work: Those with full professional education and those without,* final report. New York: NASW, undated. Mimeographed.

NASW News, November, 1964.

NASW News, October–November 1972.

NASW News, February 1973.

NASW News, January 1975.

NASW News, May, 1975.

National Conference of Lawyers and Social Workers. *Confidential and privileged communications: Guidelines for lawyers and social workers,* Publication No. 7. New York: NCLSW, August 1968.

National Education Association. *Implementing the code of ethics of the education profession and strengthening professional rights.* Washington, D.C.: NEA, June 1964.

National Federation of Societies for Clinical Social Work. Ethical standards of clinical social workers. *Clinical Social Work Journal,* **2**(4), 1974, 312–315.

National Labor Relations Board v. *Jones and Laughlin Steel Corporation,* 301 U.S. 1 (1937).

National Resources Committee. The structure of controls. In R. Bendix & S. M. Lipset (Eds.), *Class, status and power.* Glencoe, Ill.: Free Press, 1953.

National Social Welfare Assembly. *Confidentiality in social service to individuals.* New York: NSWA, 1958.

New York Post, December 19, 1974.

Nichomachean ethics. Translated by W. D. Ross. In R. McKeon (Ed.), *Introduction to Aristotle.* New York: Modern Library, 1947.

Oelsner, L. Watergate and the law: Scandal prompts a call in professions for the teaching of ethics. *New York Times,* July 16, 1973.

Opinion No. 90 (1932). In American Bar Association, *Opinions of the Committee on Professional Ethics and Grievances, with the canons of professional ethics and the canons of judicial ethics.* (Rev. ed.) 1957.

Opinion No. 250, June 26, 1943. In American Bar Association, *Opinions of the Committee on Professional Ethics and Grievances, with the canons of professional ethics and the canons of judicial ethics.* (Rev. ed.) A.B.A., 1957.

Opinion No. 376 (1947). In *Opinions of the Committee on Professional Ethics of the Association of the Bar of the City of New York and the New York County Lawyers' Association.* New York: Columbia University Press, William Nelson Cromwell Foundation, 1956.

Opinion No. 626, October 7, 1942. In *Opinions of the Committee on Professional Ethics of the Association of the Bar of the City of New York and the New York County Lawyers' Association.* New York: Columbia University Press, William Nelson Cromwell Foundation, 1956.

Parsons, T. (Ed.) Translated by T. Parsons & A. M. Henderson. *Max Weber: The theory of social and economic organization.* Glencoe, Ill.: Free Press, Falcon's Wing Press, 1947.

Parsons, T. Illness and the role of the physician: A sociological perspective. *American Journal of Orthopsychiatry,* **21**(3), 1951, 452–460.

Parsons, T. *The social system.* Glencoe, Ill.: Free Press, 1951.

Parsons, T. Propaganda and social control. *Essays in sociological theory.* (Rev. ed.) Glencoe, Ill.: Free Press, 1954.

Parsons, T., & Fox, R. Illness, therapy and the modern urban American family. *Journal of Social Issues,* **8**(4), 1952, 31–44.

Pellegrino, E. D. Medicine, history, and the idea of man. *Annals of the American Academy of Political and Social Science,* **346,** March 1963, 9–20.

Pellegrino, E. D. Ethical implications in changing practice. *American Journal of Nursing,* **64**(9), 1964, 110–112.

People v. *Alfani,* 227 N.Y. 334, 125 N.E. 671 (1919).

Pepper, S. C. *Ethics.* New York: Appleton-Century-Crofts, 1960.

Pepper, S. C. *World hypotheses: A study in evidence.* Berkeley: University of California Press, 1961.

Perlman, H. H. "And gladly teach." *Journal of Education for Social Work,* **3**(1), 1967, 41–50.

Platt, J. Hierarchical growth. *Bulletin of the Atomic Scientists,* November 1970, 2–4, 46–48.

Polanyi, M. *The study of man.* Chicago: University of Chicago Press, Phoenix Books, 1963.

Pollack, I. W., & Battle, W. C. Studies of the special patient: The sentence. *Archives of General Psychiatry,* **9,** 1963, 344–350.

Pound, R. *The lawyer from antiquity to modern times.* St. Paul, Minn.: West Publishing, 1953.

Profession of social work: Code of ethics. *Encyclopedia of social work.* New York: National Association of Social Workers, 1971.

Pumphrey, M. W. *The teaching of values and ethics in social work education.* Curriculum study, Vol. 13. New York: Council on Social Work Education, 1959.

Rawls, J. *A theory of justice.* Cambridge, Mass.: Harvard University Press, Belknap Press, 1971.

Reader, G. C. Basic mechanisms: Selective perception and alienation. *Journal of the American Medical Association,* **189**(2), 1964, 144–147.

Redlich, F. Ethical aspects of clinical observations of behavior. *Journal of Nervous and Mental Disease,* **157**(5), 1973, 313–319.

Regan, R. E., & Macartney, J. T. Professional secrecy and privileged communications. *Catholic Lawyer,* **2**(1), 1956, 3–14.

Rehr, H. Problems for a profession in a strike situation. *Social Work,* **5**(2), 1960, 22–28.

Reichert, K. Introductory remarks. Supplement to *Social Work,* **10**(4), 1965, 140–141.

Rein, M. The social service crisis. *Trans-Action,* **1**(4), 1964, 3–6, 31–32.

Rein, M. Social work in search of a radical profession. *Social Work,* **15**(2), 1970, 13–28.

Reynolds, B. C. *Learning and teaching in the practice of social work.* New York: Rinehart, 1942.

Richardson, W. P. *The law of evidence.* (8th ed.) Brooklyn, N.Y.: Jerome Prince, 1955.

Riessman, F. The "helper" therapy principle. *Social Work,* **10**(2), 1965, 27–32.

Riessman, F. *The revolution in social work: The new nonprofessional.* Report prepared for Mobilization for Youth and the Urban Studies Center, Rutgers University, New Brunswick, New Jersey, October 1963. Mimeographed.

Robinson, V. P. Is unionization compatible with social work? Address delivered to the National Coordinating Committee of Social Service Employees, Philadelphia, March 23, 1937. Mimeographed.

Rogers, A. K. *The theory of ethics.* New York: Macmillan, 1922.

Russell, B. *Power: A new social analysis.* New York: W. W. Norton, 1938.

Savage, C. Countertransference in the therapy of schizophrenics. *Psychiatry,* **24**(1), 1961, 53–60.

Schneider, I. The use of patients to act out professional conflicts. *Psychiatry,* **26**(1), 1963, 88–94.

Schorr, A. L. Policy issues in fighting poverty. *Children,* **11**(4), 1964, 127–131.

Sharaf, M. R., & Levinson, D. J. The quest for omnipotence in professional training: The case of the psychiatric resident. *Psychiatry,* **27**(2), 1964, 135–149.

Shor, J. & Sanville, J. Erotic provocations and dalliances in psychotherapeutic practice: some clinical cues for preventing and repairing therapist-patient collusions. *Clinical Social Work Journal,* **2**(2), 1974, 83–95.

Silver, H. Jewish communal services: Historical perspectives. *Journal of Jewish Communal Service,* **39**(1), 1962, 7–19.

Silver v. *Lansburgh and Bro. et al.,* 72 App. D.C. 77, 128 A.L.R. 582, 111 F. 2d. 518 (1940).

Soloveitchick, J. B. Confrontation. *Tradition,* **6**(2), 1964, 5–29.

Soyer, D. The right to fail. *Social Work,* **8**(3), 1963, 72–78.

Spiro, M. E. Social systems, personality, and functional analysis. In B. Kaplan (Ed.), *Studying personality cross-culturally.* New York: Harper & Row, 1961.

Stark, N. J. The public's concern for professional competence. *Journal of the American Medical Association,* **189**(1), 1964, 115–119.

Strauss, G. Dilemma for engineers: Union or professional society? *Monthly Labor Review,* **87**(9), 1964, 1026–1028.

Studt, E. An outline for study of social authority factors in casework. *Social Casework,* **35**(6), 1954, 231–238.

Symposium on medical education. *Journal of the American Medical Association,* **189**(1), 1964, 115–132.

Tanner, V. *Selected social work concepts for public welfare workers.* Washington, D.C.: U.S. Department of Health, Education, & Welfare, 1965.

Taylor, R. K. The social control function in casework. *Social Casework,* **39**(1), 1958, 17–21.

Thibaut, J. W., & Kelley, H. H. *Social psychology of groups.* New York: John Wiley, 1959.

Toren, N. *Social work: The case of a semi-profession.* Beverly Hills, Calif.: Sage, 1972.

Toulmin, S. E. *An examination of the place of reason in ethics.* Cambridge, England: University Press, 1950.

Towle, C. *Common human needs.* (Rev. ed.) New York: National Association of Social Workers, 1957.

Towle, C. *The learner in education for the professions: As seen in education for social work.* Chicago: University of Chicago Press, 1954.

Turner, D. A. The licensing effort—seven years later. *Social Work Journal,* **35**(2), 1954, 68–72.

United States Civil Service Commission. *Motivating employees through within-grade pay increases.* Personnel Management Series, No. 17. Washington, D.C.: U.S. Government Printing Office, November, 1965.

Vickers, G. *The art of judgment: A study of policy making.* New York: Basic Books, 1965.

Waelder, R. Symposium: Selection of criteria for the training of psychoanalytic students. III. The selection of candidates. *International Journal of Psychoanalysis,* **43,** 1962, 283–286.

Warren, E. Address presented to the Jewish Theological Seminary of America, New York City, November 11, 1962. Mimeographed.

Weber, M. Politics as a vocation. In H. H. Gerth & C. W. Mills (Eds.), *Essays in sociology.* New York: Oxford University Press, 1946.

Weintraub, W. The V.I.P. syndrome: A clinical study in hospital psychiatry. *Journal of Nervous and Mental Disease,* **138,** 1964, 181–193.

White, R. B., & Lindt, H. Psychological hazards in treating physical disorders of medical colleagues. *Diseases of the Nervous System,* **24**(5), 1963, 304–309.

Whitebook, O. E. The professional confidence in the case work relationship. *The Family,* **26**(7), 1945, 250–257.

Whitehorn, J. C. Education for uncertainty. *Perspectives in Biology and Medicine,* **7**(1), 1963, 118–123.

Wilcox, E. B. Quoted in *Check Mark,* publication of the Institute of Chartered Accountants of Ontario, Canada, No. 17, December 1964.

Wilensky, H. L. The professionalization of everyone? *American Journal of Sociology,* **70**(2), 1964, 137–158.

Wilensky, H. L., & Lebeaux, C. N. *Industrial society and social welfare.* New York: Russell Sage Foundation, 1958.

Willauer, P. B. Civil rights in labor management relations: A management viewpoint. *Annals of the American Academy of Political and Social Science,* **275,** May 1951, 140–147.

Wilson, E. K. Conformity revisited. *Trans-Action,* **2**(1), 1964, 28–32.

Wolf, A. Morality and the population explosion. In S. C. Post (Ed.), *Moral values and the superego concept in psychoanalysis.* New York: International Universities Press, 1972.

Wolff, K. R. (Trans. & ed.) *The sociology of Georg Simmel.* New York: Free Press of Glencoe, 1964.

Wolstein, B. *Transference: Its meaning in psychoanalytic therapy.* New York: Grune & Stratton, 1954.

Working definition of social work practice. *Social Work,* **3**(2), 1958, 5–8.

Yarmolinsky, A. Shadow and Substance in Politics (2): Ideas into programs. *Public Interest,* No. 2, Winter 1966, 70–79.

Yerby, A. S. The disadvantaged and health care. *American Journal of Public Health,* **56**(1), 5–9.

Youngdahl, B. Social workers—stand up and be counted. *Compass,* **28**(3), 1947, 21–24.

INDEX

Accommodation, of student, 235-236

Accountability, and freedom, 132

Accountants, and third parties, 148

Adams, M. L., on "good" behavior, 65-66

Addams, Jane, 201

"Affective neutrality," 74, 134-135

Agency, and impartiality, 127
and social worker, 171-174
and supervisor, 181-182
vs. trade unions, 201-202
See also Employer

Agency sanction, connotation of, 42

American Psychological Association, on competence, 117

Anxiety, and dependency, 75

Aristotle, on virtues, 26

Aspirations, and job descriptions, 188

Attitudes, and impartiality, 123

Autonomy, of client, 144
preservation of, 40-41
in service situation, 59

"Background fairness," 159

Baker v. Humphrey, on professional ethics, 37

Barber, B., on professions, 38

Barry, B., on "background fairness," 159
on "procedural fairness," 158

Begelman, D. A., on client rights, 86
on effectiveness, 24
on technique, 92

"Behavior" control, 73, 74

Benoit-Smullyan, E., on power, 71
on professional status, 35

Black's Law Dictionary, on fiduciary relation, 59

Boudreau, P. J., on legal regulation, 220

Breggin, P. R., on coercion, 76

Brown, J. M., on power, 70